A BLACK WOMAN'S LIFE
AND LIBERATION IN HEAVY METAL

WHAT ARE YOU DOING HERE?

LAINA DAWES

Bazillion Points

WHAT ARE YOU DOING HERE?
A Black Woman's Life and Liberation in Heavy Metal

Copyright © 2012 Laina Dawes
First printing, published in 2012 by

Bazillion Points
61 Greenpoint Ave. #504
Brooklyn, New York 11222
United States
www.bazillionpoints.com

ISBN 978-1-935950-05-9
Printed in the United States

Cover layout and design by Bruno Guerreiro
Interior design by Bazillion Points
Produced by Ian Christe
Edited by Polly Watson

Elizabeth Alexander, "The Hall of Duchess DuBarry" from *The Venus Hottentot*.
Copyright © 1990 by Elizabeth Alexander. Reprinted with the permission of
The Permissions Company, Inc., on behalf of Graywolf Press.

We can neither reflectively choose our color identity nor downplay its social significance simply by willing it to be unimportant...but our color no more binds us to send a predetermined group message to our fellow human beings than our language binds us to convey predetermined thoughts.—AMY GUTMANN

Sometimes I think nothing is simple but the feeling of pain.—LESTER BANGS

PHOTO CREDITS:

Table of Contents

Who Put That Shaven-Headed Black Woman on the Stage?

Foreword by Skin

WAS BROUGHT UP IN A HOUSE FULL OF BOB MARLEY MUSIC. I'm of Jamaican heritage, and my grandfather had a nightclub in the basement of his house. My earliest memories are of watching people dancing. None of the music I listened to when I grew older—such as Led Zeppelin, Blondie, and the Police—was allowed in my household, as it wasn't a part of our culture. All I heard was reggae and soul, so Bob Marley was my Elvis.

The first time I heard rock music it was really exciting. I felt that this new music and vibe was really *me*. I remember going to bed and having dreams that I was performing this music and visualizing myself on stage, way before it actually happened. I always knew I could sing, but I was very, very shy as a child, really scared and nervous. As I grew older I became more empowered. I started singing jazz, my first love, but I really had a rock voice. And I was clearly a rocker. I didn't like standing around, not being the center of attention, while the musicians were doing long solos.

When I started out as a rock singer, white people got me even though I was completely different. To them, I was really unique. In London within my circle of friends and associates, everybody just did everything. We didn't have the stigma of "black people do this," "white people do that," or "Asian people do this." But when it came to people outside that scene, I heard criticisms. I started to realize that what I was doing was quite hard for some people to swallow—even my family and some of my older friends.

In the very beginning I started doing backup and session work for R&B bands, which meant I had people telling me what to wear, and how I should present myself. When you are first starting out you are the most vulnerable, because you don't know the answers to many questions. Record companies seem have lots of answers; they tell you you'll sell more records and be more successful if you look like this or that. Skunk Anansie got a lot of that in the very beginning of our career. I completely ignored it. It was like water off the back of a duck. I didn't care what anyone said. Today, I do listen to people a little bit more, but if anybody starts a sentence with "You'll be more successful if you…" I just switch off.

What always appealed to me about rock music was the feeling of freedom, that I could finally be who I wanted to be and sing the music that I felt in my heart. Some black people that I met in the music industry felt that we could be stronger and better empowered if we all stayed within in the same box, but I had always relished the fact that I never belonged to any cliques, or any scenes. When you get out of that box, and challenge what black people are supposed to say and think, some feel threatened. I once got some very negative feedback from a major session singer who said, "You are not doing music for your people." That hurt, and I always remembered her comment. I had been really inspired by this woman, but now I felt she was wrong, because she was limiting what black people can achieve, and so I decided that I would always do exactly what I wanted.

As a black artist myself in Europe, even though I play music that originally came from the blues, it was quite provocative. I was a black woman with a shaven head fronting an intense rock band. I knew I was different in a positive way. When we tried to break into the American market in the mid-1990s, Skunk Anansie caused some confusion, because we had two black members and two white members. One of the members wore dreadlocks, so he was mistaken for a Rasta. People wanted to know—was our music *reggae*?

My style was really quite shocking to some people, and the music was angsty and in your face. We were messing around with all the categories. I remember once arriving at a radio station in our tour bus, and walking straight into a live-to-air broadcast. When we sat down, everybody in the station just went quiet. When the host finally spoke, he said, "As you can see, we're quite shocked to see you. There has been a big movement to get you banned from playing here." That was news to us. We had found out a few days before that our show had been moved from a 200-person capacity venue to a 2,000-capacity venue, which seemed ridiculous. We knew we weren't going to fill the place, but we thought the local booking agents must have known what they were doing.

Looking a little queasy, the radio host continued. "I think there has been a bit of misinformation circulating. The first venue refused to have you perform there. We heard you were a skinhead and your band was named Skunk-a-Nazi."

During that era, I remember going to record shops and seeing our album in the R&B section. The staff would look at the cover and just put it in that section. That happened time and time again. It seemed like every time we visited a record company we'd be forced to meet the head of urban music. A black person couldn't come in the door without meeting the lone black executive, and as a rock band we would have absolutely *nothing* to talk about with them.

America in particular was very difficult on three levels: It was difficult to be a female fronting a rock band; it was very difficult to be a black person fronting a rock band; and it was difficult to be shaven-headed and fronting a rock band. We had a lot of barriers that made us outsiders, but at the same time, those issues also brought us very strong support. We have a lot of fans who loved us passionately from the beginning, and continue to love us to this day. We always did very well in all the major cities, such as New York, Los Angeles, San Francisco, and Chicago, and had great Canadian gigs in Toronto and Montreal, too. We also got a lot of love from major American bands, such as Kid Rock, Marilyn Manson, Rage Against the

Machine, Rollins Band, Deftones, Sevendust (I later did a duet, "Licking Cream," with vocalist Lajon Witherspoon on their *Home* album), Staind, and the Red Hot Chili Peppers.

I've always tried to talk about politics from a personal angle, and all our records, including 2012's *Black Traffic*, are indicative of that. We write about our experiences with racism and social issues. I worked hard to find an individual way to express my own voice, because there are so many clichés to avoid. "Little Baby Swastikkka" from 1995's *Paranoid and Sunburnt* was written because I saw a swastika that looked like a child's first attempt. I literally thought, "Who put that baby swastika on the wall?" and that series of questions and where they led became a song about indoctrinating children into racist ideas that I think really affected a lot of people.

People are drawn to riffs and melodies, but I think songs take us to a deeper level once you start looking at the lyrics and start to see the whole story. When people reach that point—and they don't always get there right away—it has always been really important to me to put something of substance there for them. I think it that has always been one of the things that people love about Skunk Anansie; we talk about very strong personal points of view as well as relationships. The lyrics are not patronizing, and I don't constantly wag a finger at people. The audience understands that our experiences are the same as theirs. We don't put ourselves on a pedestal, telling people off with our songs. It's more like, "This happened to me— has it happened to you?" That kind of connection makes a song hit much harder.

I do feel that, due to the influence of American rap and hip hop, images of women throughout the music industry have become so much more sexualized than they were ten or fifteen years ago. Young female singers are now expected to move like tabletop dancers and pole dancers, which somebody must think is all men like. Everything has been all turned around. In Skunk Anansie's heyday, the music scene was all about strong women; now our most popular women performers are dancing around in their underwear. Though I see that more in other types of music, I sympathize with young women artists who feel that they have to adhere to those stereotypes in order to obtain success. At the same time, there are a few strong and individualistic women coming through, like Adele, Beth Ditto of the Gossip, Romy Madley Croft of the xx, Shingai Shoniwa of the Noisettes, and Samaha Sam from Paris's Shaka Ponk. So women running around in G-strings and writhing around a pole is not the only way to obtain commercial success.

The music industry is very good at pushing its ideals on women. Especially black women, who are often pushed into hypersexualized roles. It doesn't matter who we are: We are all supposed to be sexually aggressive and animalistic. I really enjoy being sexual as a performer—I'm a massive flirt onstage and in videos like "My Ugly Boy," but I feel that women watching me are comfortable and not intimidated by that. I love to feel sexy in well-fitting clothes, but that doesn't mean I have to expose loads of flesh. I personally would feel vulnerable and less empowered standing around in my underwear.

My advice to new artists is to learn every aspect of your craft from the ground up. Knowledge of the workings of the studio gives you power. If you have more power in the studio, you are much more likely to be able to express your individuality, which helps you stand out from the crowd.

Stay true to yourself and keep your own spirit. For me, the most basic and important role of an artist is to find your own original way to express yourself, something that gives you the inner confidence that helps you shine within your music. You'll be more confident writing songs and performing.

I used my intuition to choose the right people to work with me. Over the years I have learned how to read my instinct when it comes to choosing the right people to work with. This has been as important as learning how to sing. There were many occasions where I really had to stay in touch with how I felt about people and different situations. Thankfully, I chose the right manager early on, which had a huge ongoing effect on my career. She then went on to choose the right lawyer, the right live agent, the right accountant, and the right record label. Together, we found fantastic musicians, which was very lucky, as great musicians and great friends like Cass Lewis, Mark Richardson, and Ace don't fall out of the sky everyday.

All of these steps seemed like very small decisions at the time, but they have had a huge positive effect on my career. I would have had great difficulty rebounding after choosing a wrong manager during the early stages, as I would have lost the newest and freshest part of my talent. And at twenty-four years old, I was already kind of a late starter.

I urge new artists to stay as individual and original as they can be. It's important to try and do your own thing. I place the highest importance on staying connected with the truest part of myself, and not moving away from my core being. When I haven't done this, I have felt that I was someone else, like I was being fake. Good things stopped happening to me if I moved too far away from who I really was.

But keep in mind, doing your own thing might mean that you'll never be successful. Not everybody can be. Maybe you just haven't got *it*—in that case you need to move on and not waste your time.

There is only one Bono, only one Gaga, and only one Skin.

July 2012

Introduction

WHEN I DISCUSS BLACK WOMEN in the metal, hardcore, and punk scenes, the most common response from people who don't know me is a three-second pause, and then: *Huh?* Some will stutter and avoid eye contact. People often do not know how to react, and they struggle to find something to say that doesn't sound either offensive or dismissive.

Any reaction is fine and understandable—up to a point, anyway. I know by now that they don't know any black female friends or musicians who are into the music. It's not that we, black women, shouldn't be there. But why aren't we?

Metal, hardcore, and punk music are widely perceived as giving a voice to the voiceless, hoisting up music and a culture for outsiders who cannot or choose not to conform to societal standards. Many find an emotional anchor lacking in other aspects of their lives, in what is often thought to be a community based on shared musical preferences for loud, abrasive sounds and equally loud and abrasive attitudes.

When I began writing this book, I reread Lester Bangs's excellent essay "The White Noise Supremacists" for the umpteenth time. In the piece, first published in the *Village Voice* in 1979, the late music journalist writes about the development of his awareness on race while being immersed in the '70s-era punk scene in New York City. While stunned by the casual racism of his friends and acquaintances, Bangs admits to his own racist gaffes;

using racial epithets and stereotypes for comedic shock value: "I thought absolutely nothing of going to parties with people like David Ruffin and Bobby Womack where I'd get drunk, maul the women, and improvise blues songs along the lines of 'Sho' wish ah wuz a nigger, then mah dick'd be bigger,' and of course they all laughed. It took years before I realized what an asshole I'd been, not to mention how lucky I was to get out of there with my white hide intact." He realizes that if people do not take racism seriously, nothing will really change.

Bangs never mentions black women in the essay. While I didn't really expect him to, I had always wondered about that blind spot. Admittedly, Bangs was writing from his own white, privileged background and, despite his honesty, was more focused on his own self-absorbedness than on the perspectives of the people at the receiving end of "nigger." He briefly mentions the experiences of his "black" friends, people with a secondary role in the essay, and their observations about the '70s punk scene resonated with me as a heavy metal devotee. Bangs relays the words of his black friend Richard Pinkston: "'When I go to CBGB's I feel like I'm in East Berlin. I don't mind liberal guilt if it gets me in the restaurant, even if I know the guy still hates me in his mind. But it's like down there they're *striving* to be offensive however they can, so it's more vocal and they're freer. It's semi-mob thinking.'"

Pinkston's perspective was interesting to me. I have been in situations similar to Bangs's alcohol- and drug-soaked party where he played his "nigger disco shit." I'm sure many people have been in a situation, regardless of race or ethnicity, where they were affected by uncomfortable silence or conspiratorial laughter after a racially awkward event. But we have never really had the opportunity to talk about it, how it hurt us or at least, made us question our friendships. Those racial gaffes—that silent yet thick tension centered around being in a social space where your presence is considered an anomaly—still occur in today's white-dominated musical scenes.

I was about nine years old when Bangs's article was first published.

Rereading this essay over the years, I always wondered what it would have been like to be my twenty-one-year-old self in that era, someone who simply wanted to go to CBGB or one of the popular haunts of the day. I imagined having to navigate spaces where I might run into someone like Ron Asheton of the Stooges, who, as Bangs described, wore swastikas, iron crosses, and jackboots onstage. As a black person and as a woman, I may not have been welcome, as the stares and a thickening air would have made my presence there uncomfortable for everyone. I would like to think that if a button-pushing punk singer started spouting racially offensive drivel, I would run up on the stage and violently insert my boot into the perpetrator's mouth. In all likelihood, I would not. Honestly, I have no idea what I would do. Black guitarist Ivan Julian, a founding member of Richard Hell and the Voidoids, told Bangs that "regardless of how much people might have in common, they still draw away."

Today the scenario is not hard for me to imagine. The '70s punk scene sounds very similar to contemporary society, where situations occur that confound me in my very real life. We still sweep discussions under the proverbial rug about why we inherently feel that people should listen to music and participate in subcultures based on their skin color. Among friends and coconspirators, I might grumble and complain, but the fact remains that full inclusion within the metal, hardcore, and punk communities remains incomplete.

I'll be the first to admit that, like any other book, *What Are You Doing Here?* is partly self-serving. I wanted to find other black women like me: metal, hardcore, and punk fans and musicians who were rabid about the music and culture and adamant about asserting their rightful place as black women within those scenes. I wanted to find other women who put aside the cultural baggage that dictates that we must listen to certain types of music, and simply enjoy the music that influenced us, not just as black women, but as individuals who grew up in an era when, thanks to technology, a large variety of music was accessible and available to everyone. I found many black women and have shared their stories, but I also realize there is still a lot of work to be done.

This book was inspired by various projects I worked on from 1997 to 2008. In university I penned op-ed pieces—well, more like rants—for my university newspaper. I wrote and produced a radio documentary for the CBC, the Canadian Broadcast Corporation, on women in rock 'n' roll. I also spoke at a number of conferences on racial identity in rock and metal culture at music conferences in Canada and the U.S. In 2004, I coproduced and moderated a one-day symposium in Toronto on the representation of black men and women in the rock scenes. We invited black alternative artists such as K-OS; Murray Lightburn from the Dears; James Spooner, the director of the documentary *Afro-Punk: The Rock 'n' Roll Nigger Experience*; and journalist Kandia Crazy Horse, editor of *Rip it Up: The Black Experience in Rock 'n' Roll*, to speak about the joys and the pain of being a black artist in a predominantly white scene.

While the musical artists were performing alternative genres of music, there were still enough black cultural signifiers in the music for them to be accepted within urban media outlets. Because I had been primarily influenced by music that came of out of the New Wave of British Heavy Metal—or NWOBHM—and thrash metal, I have pretty puritanical views on what is considered "rock" and "alternative." To me, a hip hop group that happens to add some guitar sounds does not automatically rate as a rock band. Yet when I talk about guitar-driven, straight-up metal, I feel like that music was looked down upon.

After a brief stint as a hip hop critic when I was younger, very unsure, and thought that no one would hire me to write about metal for a living, I started writing about alternative and rock music along with race and social justice issues for some local publications. After my essay on the British alternative rock/metal band Skunk Anansie, featuring the black female vocalist Skin, was published in the 2007 anthology *Marooned: The Next Generation of Desert Island Discs*, I focused totally on the metal scene, writing for such national print and online publications as *Metal Edge*, *Hellbound*, *Exclaim!*, and *Consequence of Sound*. After being offered a photo pass to a 2009 Metallica concert, I took a chance, bought a DLSR camera, and started shooting bands in Canada and the U.S.

What Are You Doing Here? investigates how black women musicians and fans navigate the metal, hardcore, and punk music genres that are regularly thought of as inclusive spaces and centered on a community spirit, but fail to block out the race and gender issues that exist in the outside world. I started by writing about the metal scene, my preferred culture and the sphere I know most about. However, once I learned of the level of involvement of black fans and musicians in the hardcore and punk music scenes, I brought them into the book as well. While the music might differ, the experiences of the black female musicians and fans are similar. Black women face resistance to their participation as fans and musicians, questions about their racial and cultural identity, and resentment when they assert their rightful place within the scenes in which they are involved.

Racism, as it affects lifers in the metal scene like me, is not the primary reason for this book. The point is expressing the experiences of black women musicians, fans, writers, photographers, and record label owners to assert their individual *freedom*. This is about the freedom to listen to and enjoy the music we choose, music that, while not as vilified as it was thirty years ago, still gets a bad rep. I refer to freedom as a mechanism to find what we need in music, emotionally and physically, and to be able to actively participate in the music scene we prefer. For musicians, *freedom* means the ability to build a career playing the music in a way that speaks to them, and being able to obtain opportunities to record and tour, based on their talent and determination and not on their race or gender.

Twenty years ago, cultural theorists–turned–heavy metal authors Deena Weinstein (*Heavy Metal: The Music and Its Culture*) and Robert Walser

(*Running With The Devil: Power, Gender, and Madness in Heavy Metal Music*) wrote about the involvement of disenfranchised young men—and a few women—in the metal scene. Their conclusions about why these men are drawn to the music as an energetic, defiant alternative to conforming to societal norms certainly also apply to black women—even more so. While there is a shared sense of metal repaying some of the world's unfairness in relation to social and economical class differences, the addition of racial and gender inequality adds extra need for black women to find ways to express themselves and their individuality.

Since young men are still considered the majority in the metal scene, their experience commonly defines the entire heavy metal experience. Despite the class discrimination and the stereotypes they face, at least men can generally be assured that they won't be criticized at a metal show for their gender, ethnicity, or class status.

This book is about black women finding liberation in metal and hardcore, and being able to express their individuality and simply be themselves as active participants in the metal and punk scenes. Bangs writes that participants within the late-'70s punk scene were looking for liberation from societal pressure, as he describes Richard Hell's vision of "a bunch of people finally freed by the collapse of all values to reinvent themselves, to make art statements of their whole lives." To me, that desire for freedom and liberation is the same desire conveyed by the teenagers hanging out in the parking lot before the Judas Priest concert in the 1986 documentary *Heavy Metal Parking Lot*. These kids could be cousins of the suburban white kids who throw spontaneous hardcore shows in abandoned houses or their parents' basements. The music is energetic and alive, encouraging people give themselves over to the experience while surrounded by like-minded people. It's about finding and creating a voice for the voiceless. The reasons why people use a musical genre and culture as a way to escape from the rigors of everyday life, or even just to *feel* in a world that desperately pushes conformity, is the same. The lure in listening to metal is to *feel* free, to escape from reality, even just for the length of a four-minute song.

Being able to assert my individuality within the metal scene was extremely crucial. Social invisibility, something that I distinctly felt, being a black girl being raised in an all-white, rural environment steeped with racial inequalities, didn't go away when I moved away at eighteen to a larger, more culturally diverse city. The music let me scream and vent my frustration at times when no one wanted to listen to how I felt. As an adult, I have moved from being a metal listener to working as a metal music journalist and photographer. I continue to enjoy it and still use it when I need to vent.

Throughout my preteen and early adult years I learned that women—particularly black women—are not supposed to show anger, through words or actions. Not only is anger an unattractive quality in a society that prefers women of all cultural and ethnic backgrounds to be gentle and passive, but for black women, being loud and angry harkens back to racial stereotypes that have deterred our social and economical progress. The subtle but emotionally damaging thought that because of the perceived allowance for black folks to be free after a turbulent history of slavery and racial economic and social oppression, we *must* be silent and thankful to be allowed to participate in everyday society, is oppressive. However, during the process of writing this book, talking to women in the metal, hardcore, and punk scenes and thinking about my personal interactions with others, I discovered that despite the societal issues that can deter black women from actively participating, either by personal choice or because of the actions of others, the extreme music scenes can offer a community that encourages people to unlock and express emotions of passion, anger, hurt, rage, and joy, which we tend to push down, in a manner that does not harm others or themselves. Most importantly, it has also encouraged women involved in these musical scenes to assert and appreciate their individuality.

N

The emotional ramifications of the pressure to conform and to suppress feelings of inequality based on race, sexism, and class have been well documented in both fiction and nonfiction books by Patricia Hill Collins, Alice Walker, Toni Morrison, and many other prominent black women writers. All feature recurring themes of social invisibility, and the struggle to assert identity in a world that didn't really want to recognize it. The many stories I've heard from black girlfriends and acquaintances, and what I have gone through myself, experiences with depression and drug abuse, mirror the fictionalized accounts from these notable authors. For me and for the black women fans I interviewed, heavy music helped us through periods of personal strife, even when we secretly wondered how we didn't lose our sanity. The loud, and sometimes angry music let us vent our frustrations, yell and scream and express emotions that are not exactly acceptable to express in the pubic sphere.

The music also helped us channel our anger into something positive, and our insistence in not letting people deter us from being active in our chosen music scenes is an example of how we've shaped our own individuality by doing what we want to do. As human beings, we have the right to do and be who we are. However, while music can be therapeutic, it would be nice if it could simply be used for enjoyment, not to exorcise the damage that the outside world can do to our inner selves.

In his forward for the anthology *Rip It Up: The Black Experience in Rock 'n' Roll*, Greg Tate muses that despite the documented history of black involvement in rock music "I remain amazed that as simple an act as a young black man or woman deciding not to sing straight-up reggae, blues, or hip hop can still get people's panties in a knot."

In 2000, Keidra Chaney wrote the popular essay "Sister Outsider Headbanger" for *Bitch* magazine. She discussed not only the difficulties of metal fandom from a black female perspective, but also how it clashed with cultural authenticity: "After all," she wrote, "conventional wisdom holds that 'normal' black people do not listen to heavy metal. Like decaffeinated coffee, a black female metalhead is something that doesn't make sense to a lot of people. What could I possibly find appealing about heavy metal, seeing as how it didn't reflect my life experience or cultural identity in any tangible way?"

So the lack of support for black women metal musicians and fans from friends, family, and "black-centric" media outlets also concerns me—as if being a black woman in a predominantly white and male music scene wasn't hard enough.

In writing *What Are You Doing Here?* I wondered whether the book would be misconstrued as an "I hate whitey" exposé of heavy metal's baser elements. I also had some concerns about offending people, or painting black communities in a negative light by making sweeping generalizations, but the women and men I interviewed were honest with their feelings. I slowly learned how to be honest with mine. I am confident that this book will help the family and friends of black women fans and musicians understand the music, and yes, acknowledge the troubling aspects of the metal and hardcore and punk scenes. Hopefully, through the stories of women who are currently active there, they will also appreciate the positives about getting involved within these music scenes.

I hope some important points come across to you, the reader. First, about the communal aspects of the metal scene: Many of the white musicians and record label employees I talked to feel that the visual image of the musicians is less important than the music, which is far more intricate and demands more technical proficiency than other popular musical genres. So in theory, people shouldn't care about the ethnicity or gender of the musician, and metal fans should be less likely to discriminate based on those factors. However, as I learned from the interviews I conducted with black women in the metal, hardcore, and punk scenes, the insular utopia of the metal community is filled with problematic issues that stand in the way of more active participation.

Based on my experiences as a journalist and photographer, and also on the stories told by some of the interviewees, sexual and racial stereotyping and threats of physical harm can limit the participation of black women fans. Even without being surrounded by "vocal" clubgoers "striving to be offensive," as Richard Pinkston experienced when entering CBGB, sometimes you can become so uncomfortable at a show, owing to the tension there, that you want to leave. Some of the women interviewed for this book avoid shows altogether because they want to avoid potential verbal and physical confrontations, especially in cases where the band members themselves are rumored to hold racist views.

One of the most common complaints I have heard from young black metal, hardcore, and punk fans is that they do not know of any black musicians and do not have any friends or even acquaintances who want to attend concerts with them. Some of the women I talked to purchase the music, but only listen to it in the privacy of their bedrooms, and while they acknowledged the positive aspects of the way in which the music impacts their lives, they were very hesitant in entering public spaces that were largely populated by whites to hear the music performed live. Some were fearful of being at the receiving end of racial slurs or getting physically attacked, and of what their friends or family might think if they knew what music they listened to. Because of this, they do not want to go to shows and thus can't enjoy the scene as much as they could.

So here is another point I hope this book drives home: Although race and gender can hinder participation, both can still be very positive within the extreme music scenes. The metal scene has served as an environment in which black women musicians have been able to assert themselves as performers. Black women fans have been able to navigate the scenes they are involved in and to benefit from them, as they have found communities of people who share the same interests that they do. I'm hoping that this book will encourage black women and men by revealing the strength and enthusiasm of the people out there actively involved in the scene as musicians, fans, and industry workers. Despite some difficult experiences, they have persevered and made it easier for other black people to actively participate.

All people, regardless of gender, race, and class, can be a part of both extreme music and black-centric musical scenes. By looking at the history of black women musicians, from the blues era to modern-day popular music, *What Are You Doing Here?* reveals the common thread of strength and determination among black women musicians in male-dominated music industries. We have a track record of resilience against all the obstacles put in our paths. While it sometimes seems unfair that, despite the social and economical advances within North American life, there are still struggles for legitimacy, there is always a way to survive and thrive.

Many of the metal, hardcore, and punk bands described in this book exist outside of the mainstream, operating with much lower profiles than marquee-name metal and punk acts, such as Metallica, Iron Maiden, Megadeth, Ozzy Osbourne, the Clash, or the Sex Pistols. The niche bands and up-and-comers are featured in print publications like *Decibel*, the UK's *Metal Hammer* and *Terrorizer*, and the publication I wrote for before its demise in 2009, *Metal Edge*. Plus, there are online publications like *Brave Words & Bloody Knuckles*, *Crustcake*, *MetalSucks*, *Invisible Oranges*, *Metal Underground*, *Brooklyn Vegan*, and *Hellbound* that regularly post on happenings within the scene.

As a journalist I write and review albums from underground bands, and I wanted to talk to women who were also in those particular scenes, because I think attending shows in the extreme music scene, many of which are held in relatively small venues and have limited promotion, requires more dedication and tolerance than attending a stadium concert. The attendees at mainstream metal shows are slightly more diverse in terms of age, class, and ethnicity, just due to the sheer numbers involved and because their music is transmitted through widely accessible radio formats and the larger video channels. People who are interested in underground bands have to put in a bit more legwork into attending shows and finding the music.

As attending live shows is a crucial aspect in metal, hardcore, and punk culture, discussing the dynamics between audience members was critical and for me the most rewarding part of the book. I was really excited to interview fans. I understand the fear of losing friends who feel that, because you hang out at shows or have nonblack friends who are also into the same music, you prefer the company of whites over your black friends and communities. During the research phase and the writing of this book, I lost a few friends myself.

I originally had a hard time finding many black people around me in Ontario and Quebec into metal, and the handful I talked to were generally reluctant to openly discuss their fandom. Of course, that reticence only confirmed to me that something warranted further investigation here. I looked to American fans and found many working musicians who seemed willing to simply be themselves, refusing the cultural stereotyping that pressured them to perform black-centric music. In addition, I've come into contact with black British and African metal fans and musicians, including the burgeoning Botswana metal bands Skinflint and Wrust and the female-fronted thrash metal band Sasamuso from Madagascar. More black folks are actively participating in the metal scene and enjoying the music than I originally thought. Still, I wondered if their experiences matched my own.

Even with the bolder American fans I still encountered the issue of outing. While researching this book, I met people in many different ways, some through friends and colleagues, others who contacted me directly after reading my published articles or my blog, *Writing Is Fighting*. Few people had a problem sending me a quick introductory message, but some did not want to have an extended conversation about their private lives or musical tastes. There were also a few who openly admitted that they did not want their friends or families to find out about their metal interests.

However I was dumbfounded when a small handful of well-established black women working as rock musicians, backing big-name artists, or working behind the scenes in the music industry flat-out refused to be interviewed. I suspect that they did not want to talk about racial and sexual politics for fear that their white colleagues would be turned off, or perhaps they were afraid that all the hard work they had done to earn a place in the rock or metal scene would unravel. One thing that became evident was an acute but unspoken awareness of their difference in the scene. To me, they seemed to think that if they didn't publicly voice the undeniable fact that they were black, perhaps those around them would ignore their ethnicity.

I realized a lot about myself through writing this book, starting with how extremely difficult it can be to simply be yourself outside of the societal norms based on gender and ethnicity that have dictated how we are supposed to be, act, and see the world. The resistance from others to my writing this book was at times excruciatingly painful. I learned to acknowledge and cultivate my own emotional needs—to enjoy the thrill of discovering new music and finding and befriending like-minded people, while also protecting my vulnerable side. I found the limits of my temper and my patience. I also learned that others rely on the way I identify myself in order to make sense of their own experiences, and I came to recognize the pressure that has put on me in terms of how I choose to live my life. But I have to say that the women (and the men) I talked to during the course of writing this book made me a stronger and more courageous person than I originally thought I could ever be.

1. Canadian Steel

I WAS BORN IN 1969 and adopted at six months old. I grew up in a house on the outskirts of Kingston, Ontario, a small city primarily known as home to the top-tier Queen's University and also to one of the largest maximum-security prisons in Canada. Until I moved to Toronto at eighteen, there was only one AM radio station and one FM channel that played popular music in the area. My music preference was developed through those broadcasts, from my parents' record collection, and from what my neighbors and schoolmates were listening to.

Though how I grew up—as a black child in a white household—isn't that common, I gravitated toward metal in the same way many people of my generation did. Partly because of the era, and also because there were a lot of older teenage kids around, I heard a lot of rock music. My parents also collected what are now considered the seminal albums from popular artists such as the Beatles, the Eagles, the Steve Miller Band, Linda Ronstadt, and Carly Simon. There were many classical musicians on my father's side of the family, so classical music was played often in our house, interspersed with a few albums from Scott Joplin, Stevie Wonder, Aretha Franklin, Cleo Laine, and Roberta Flack.

The 1970s and 1980s, my formative years, brought a huge transformation in technology. Personal computers for middle-income families and Sony Walkman cassette players did not exist until I was in high school. In 1981, when MTV was launched in the U.S., I was spending my Saturdays at Studio 801, the local roller rink, dancing to Michael Jackson's *Off the Wall*. We didn't have access to MTV in Canada, unless you knew someone with a huge satellite dish and a lot of money, so Studio 801 was a great attraction. Kids gathered around to watch the "Thriller" video when it premiered in 1983. Compact discs emerged when I was in my early twenties, and by then I was able to afford cable television on my own.

When I wanted to hear music outside of my parents' records, I turned on the radio. The music seemed so valuable. My siblings and I would capture it on pseudo mixtapes by leaning our cassette recorder against the speakers, turning off the tape when commercials began, then waiting patiently until the music started again. Canadian Top 40 stations played a diverse selection of music, including mandatory Canadian content such as Rush, Triumph, Trooper, Helix, Lee Aaron, Loverboy, the Tragically Hip, Blue Rodeo, and lots of Bryan Adams. Today's stations are focused on particular genres, but back then, CKLC, the most popular station in Kingston, Ontario, would play Kool & the Gang one minute and the Rolling Stones the next.

I lived in a rural area where several of the neighbors had teenage sons who were into classic metal. I heard lots of Black Sabbath, and I remember that classic riff from Deep Purple's "Smoke on the Water" wafting through my open bedroom window on hot summer nights. The boys, while intimidating, also excited me because of their rough exteriors. I wanted to be more like them than a frightened little girl—even though their mean-spirited racial slurs indicated that I would never be one of them. Still, I gravitated toward their music. My older sister's friends had turned her on to AC/DC, the Clash, and the Violent Femmes. Listening to a variety of music didn't seem like a big deal in my household.

I'm tempted to say that growing up before the Internet and without the constant bombardment of information via too-many-to-count cable television channels forced the listener to go out and find the music that she liked. Because of that, music was valuable, a physical entity in which emotional attachments were formed. I treated my collection of albums and, later, cassette tapes, and after that, CDs, like gold. That music served as a soundtrack to the formation of my emotional and intellectual maturity.

There was not a unique musical genre created by black Canadians that impacted the world on a par with blues music from the United States. But the music from the Caribbean, the culturally rich soca, reggae, and calypso, served as a reminder of the countries that many new Canadians had left behind in the search for economic prosperity. They not only remained a signifier of "back home" but also allowed immigrants a way to retain their identity after leaving a country that was predominantly black for a nation where they were now a minority.

In the United States, the cultural significance of music among African slaves and black immigrants from Caribbean countries was also important in keeping cultural signifiers alive. "In North America, you have a group of people in which so much was done specifically to sever us from our past culture," says Brooklyn singer and guitarist Tamar-kali. "In the Caribbean, whether it's Cuba, Puerto Rico, the Dominican Republic, Jamaica, or Trinidad, there's so much retention in terms of music and their culture. Whether people want to identify as African or not, they are still dancing to those African rhythms. In America, drums were taken away. We don't really have any of the lingo or the language left, and some of that for American immigrants has to do with how the Spanish or the British who colonized these countries said, 'Look, you can be a part of our Empire.'"

"We have never had a revolution here, where there was segregation and we had to support each other," says Saidah Baba Talibah, a Canadian-born singer who was part of the Toronto-based, hard rock/funk group Blaxäm. Her mother, renowned jazz singer Salome Bey, immigrated to Canada from the States in 1964. "Canadians do not value music created on Canadian soil, like black Americans do gospel and blues music. We have our circle of friends, and friends of friends, but we have never been forcibly segregated into groups. The idea of listening to something outside of music that is racially coded is dictated more on: 'How are they are going to look at me?'"

While my immediate family didn't really care, I grew up feeling a palpable tension from the outside world in listening and getting involved in white music. Black parents feared that if their children got involved in an overwhelmingly white scene, that might lead to them forgetting their 'blackness.' "It's 'cause your family is white," my black friends would inform me as a teenager when I told them what band I was listening to on my Walkman, or when I explained the meaning of my Black Flag or Cult T-shirt.

Heavy metal music, like rock 'n' roll and country, had a reputation for being identified with racists. Because my adoptive family did not have an issue with what I listened to, I thought nothing of doing exactly what the other kids my age were doing: listening to and enjoying the music that was being played on the radio and spending my Saturdays at the roller rink with my white friends. Many of the black kids of my generation had a problem with that.

Rap and hip hop music hit Kingston via bootlegged cassette tapes from American relatives of my black schoolmates. When that happened, I temporarily found a de facto black family where I was welcomed simply because of the color of my skin, but I knew that it wasn't enough. I was in high school when rap music first emerged, and the music and its culture did bring the very small population of black kids together. We bonded over lyrics about racial injustice. There was joy in realizing that we shared the same experiences, even though those experiences seemed to focus on trying to maintain one's sanity while dealing with police harassment, racial discrimination, poverty, and crime. Sure, the American rap artists resided in a whole different world than we did, but the commonality of anger and frustration expressed within the lyrics was exciting. When Salt-N-Pepa, Run-DMC, and Public Enemy videos appeared on MTV, the joy of seeing young black faces on television doing something different was exciting.

I eventually learned that in order to fit in, it was best not to divulge my musical preferences, not to talk about the posters of Judas Priest's K. K. Downing on my bedroom walls, and to keep my impressive collection of hard rock magazines to myself. In my late teens, boyfriends would drag me to calypso, reggae, and soca clubs, somehow trying to "blacken" me up. I also got involved with a number of black cultural organizations to try and "blacken" myself up, thinking that if I could know what I was, maybe then I would be happy and the criticism would stop. But while I also loved R&B, rap, and later hip hop, my true love was metal.

Thankfully, the older I got, the more I dug in my heels, and eventually I no longer felt that in order to find myself I had to surround myself with black culture. Most importantly, I learned that in order to maintain my sanity and love myself for whom I was, I had to be me—whether I lost my "black pass" or not. But the balancing act was hard and sometimes continues to be a struggle—between wanting others to accept me, and knowing that ultimately, I have to accept myself.

The American women I've met and interviewed for this book had a different experience relationship to their black identity than I did growing up in Canada, which affected how music influenced their racial awareness. While the first black person arrived in Canada as early as 1603, black immigration to Canada happened in successive waves. From the late 1820s until 1861, African slaves seeking refuge from the United States streamed into Nova Scotia via the Underground Railroad. One hundred years later in 1962, a lift on immigration barriers brought an influx of people from Caribbean countries to Ontario.

Black Canadians played an important role in building the country, toiling as railroad, mill, and postal workers, and providing domestic services. Slavery, while present in Canada, did not have the same historical and psychological impact it did south of the border. Canadians were not kinder or gentler than our friends in the U.S.; the radical seasonal climate in certain parts of the country simply made slavery not economically viable. I didn't even know that slavery even existed in Canada, mostly in Quebec, until I was an adult and in university.

The pressure to assimilate in Canada made many immigrants of color feel that they should not bite the hand that presumably fed them. My black friends' parents did not openly complain about systemic, institutional, and overt racism, as they felt their employers and landlords would tell them to go back to their own countries. After all, they'd come to Canada by choice, for the most part. Aside from the economic disparities and lack of educational opportunities that made people want to flee their native countries, there was no force involved, either.

A few black families eventually moved to Kingston to work at the prison, the largest in Canada, one of the large manufacturing plants, the research hospitals, or the university. During that immigration wave, from the mid-1960s to the late 1970s, many black families were told that to succeed in their immigration bid, they would have to reside in the smaller Canadian cities and rural areas. Workers were needed in rural areas. What the Immigration Canada bureau didn't acknowledge—or care about, for that matter—was that these new Canadians would have benefited more in the larger, multicultural cities such as Montreal, Quebec, Toronto, and Ottawa. In Eastern Ontario, people were not used to seeing brown faces; they made the transition to Canada a lot more difficult.

I always thought that the parents of my black female friends were more concerned than the families of my white friends with making sure that their children excelled in school, dressed appropriately, and did not publicly embarrass themselves. Because of the very small black population in my hometown, the groupthink mentality prevailed as far as adhering to traditional values and manners. Black people wanted to be perceived as hard workers and good contributors to the fabric of the country, and the parents of my friends placed an emphasis on that, most likely after being on the receiving end of racially coded remarks from their coworkers. They wanted to raise children who would excel academically, contribute to Canadian society, and, most importantly, not embarrass the "race."

My small group of black girlfriends made me understand that their parents, who immigrated to Canada as adults, did not encourage individualism or the expression of what they wanted to do or to be outside of what was considered the norm. Black families held on to the traditions of the countries they had left with an iron fist for several reasons: Primarily, the music, the food, and the strict—sometimes devoutly religious—upbringing common in colonized countries served as reminders of where they came from.

There were also black girls who had a passion for music, dance, and visual art, but they were persuaded to get jobs that were perceived to be more secure and sensible. While it made sense that parents would be concerned about their children ending up as penniless artists, there seemed to be more concern about the embarrassment that the parents might feel telling their black friends, families, and acquaintances—many of whom were immigrants themselves—that their children were not taking advantage of all the country could offer. Supporting their children in artistic pursuits might make them look like unfit parents who not only did not care about their kids, but also were indifferent to their cultures and communities.

"Perhaps the friction I had in my family was due to that they expected me to do better with my education," says Canadian Yvonne Ducksworth, singer for seminal Berlin punk band Jingo de Lunch, about her decision to embark on a career as a musician. "I've encountered animosity from certain members of my family on my father's side, the black side. But my mother's side, the white side of my family, taught me that I should do what I do best, to do what I love."

In a country where the black population was small, the extra hurdles black female musicians needed to jump over in order to promote their careers were and still are many. "There is still the chitlin circuit in the States. Canada has never had a chitlin circuit," Talibah adds, referring to venues such as New York City's famed Apollo Theater and Chicago's Regal Theater that are known as welcoming incubators for black talent to play before African-American audiences. "People outside Canada have a dream. And then they go after the next dream and then the next goal after that. Here, maybe it's the whole mentality coming from the Caribbean and working really hard, making a change, getting here and then, saying to their Canadian-born children: 'Why do you want to mess around being an artist? Why don't you get a real job?'" The assumption remains that making music is about avoiding a "real" career, with little regard for the value of freedom of expression.

At the same time, that shield of tradition was thought to guard against the racial stereotypes that immigrants imagined they had brought with them. If people saw that you were religious, conservative, and dressed and talked with a British colonialist sensibility, then you couldn't be like the savages or ignoramuses they had heard justified slavery in America.

Laura Nicholls was involved in Toronto's punk scene in the 1980s and also grew up in predominantly white environment in Canada. Emigrating from London as a child in the 1970s, she moved with her family to a series of small Ontario towns and suburbs surrounding the greater Toronto area. "Black people weren't familiar to me. They were familiar in that we shared some physical characteristics, but they weren't like me. I felt really scared of black people in a way, as I thought I wouldn't be black enough, but I eventually realized that was my problem and it wasn't their problem.

"But when I was younger I think it created conflict, and much later, I really regretted how I initially felt. One of the things I really regretted was that I had courage in doing some things, but I didn't feel comfortable with my own people, and in hindsight, that makes me sad."

While I was never fearful of black folks as a kid, I was fearful of them thinking that I was weird, so I understand Nicholls's feelings of inferiority around them. I grew up knowing nothing about my biological family or the country where I was conceived. For the most part, my black girlfriends' families didn't like me and didn't trust my family, as they couldn't understand why a white family would volunteer to adopt black children.

Even though my parents were white, from an early age I understood that you were truly black if you listened and enjoyed the music from the Caribbean. Moreover, if you knew how to dance to the music and your family regularly cooked and enjoyed the food popular in your home country, it meant that you were part of a community that for many also served as a cultural signifier. You might not feel that you completely belonged in the white suburbs, but there was a community nearby that would always welcome you.

One of the great benefits—or hardships, depending on what you believe—of being black and adopted into a white family is that you are an accidental infiltrator: I was like the title of the satirical 1973 civil rights film, *The Spook Who Sat by the Door*. I was able to observe how "they" lived and because of that there was an expectation about how my life was going to go, that I was going to be treated exactly like them. What probably messed me up was that there was a lot of confusion when that didn't happen. As my two older white brothers and little sister were allowed to do what they wanted with their lives with no judgment from the outside world, the same wasn't true for me or my older sister, who is biracial and was adopted two years before me. Expectations for my white siblings were high. I wish I could say the same for my sister and me.

The world outside of our home saw that while my siblings and I were raised in the same home, we were not the same, and therefore we were treated accordingly. "Why can't I just be like them?" was a common thought for me during my preteen years. In later years i thought that when the criticism I got from my black friends about my music preferences made me feel like I wasn't black enough, and when white people made me feel like I was *too* black. I felt as though, in order to make both groups more comfortable, I should abandon my true self and behave as nearly everyone expected a black person would.

I had friends who experienced the same feelings of alienation that I did. For them, it manifested in serious depression and drug, alcohol, or sexual addictions, often brought on by abusive family members or family friends who took out their own emotional troubles on them. In other cases, the acting-out emerged when, desperate to be seen as just as desirable as the popular girls in our 98 percent white high school, some willingly submitted to sexual relationships, hoping to capture what it was like to be perceived the same way their desirable white female classmates were. Instead, they mistook the attention from white boys as leading to something more than a random sexual encounter. Meanwhile, the racialized sexual stereotypes that their parents warned them about, such as being sexually available, took hold.

I watched these women self-destruct, and, more than once, I watched them tell their parents about abuse or problems at school, only to see those problems swept under the rug within their homes. Such reactions left them feeling that somehow they must be at fault, especially because what happened when they confided in their parents didn't mirror what they saw on after-school TV specials. Obviously, victims of abuse are found within both genders and across all ethnicities, but I saw a correlation between the abuse and self-abuse among those who were bullied and mistreated because of their racial ethnicity. Infuriatingly, their abuse was perceived as less relevant: *Black girls are naturally hypersexual. Black girls are stupid, docile, and not as sexually virtuous as white girls. No one wants them—they just want to fuck them.*

Regardless of skin color or gender, finding one's individuality within any high school environment is challenging. I have always wondered how my friends lives' would have changed if they had found a way to let the frustrations out through artistic ventures instead of letting them destroy their self-esteem.

N

I remember seeing a divide in the way in which my love of metal was perceived by my schoolmates. While my black friends criticized me, my white male high school friends didn't bat an eye. These guys ranged in social status from the heshers to the jocks to the popular kids who had a U2 tribute band. To them I was simply another teen into the same music that they were—if maybe a bit more obsessively—and so our shared interest led to friendship. Their own families didn't seem to have a problem with their musical choices. After all, white people were used to pursuing their musical interests with little controversy. "White people get to choose. They get to define themselves," explains Laura Nicholls. "They can listen to whatever, and they are still white. Being black means that a lot of white people think that they have a right to define you, but I knew at a very young age that I was going to define myself."

For other women it wasn't that easy, as they got it from both sides. Nicholls tells the story of being invited to a house party as a teenager. "They were playing Earth, Wind and Fire. I grew up in a small suburb and I was the only black girl there. This girl walked into the party, and I recognized her because she went to my high school. She saw me, looked at me, and she said, 'Oh they're playing nigger music.' I thought to myself, 'Talk. Keep talking.' I could see her life. Maybe she'll meet a guy and maybe he'll beat the shit out of her. And maybe she'll end up on welfare and maybe she won't. Her life was written all over her face, and my life wasn't."

After talking to Nicholls, in hindsight I realized she could have been talking about me, unless that old insecurity creeping in about my presence in the metal scene was acting up again: "Don't forget who you are," she said. "Even though you are accepted now, you're still a nigger. Behave yourself accordingly. I was so grateful to that girl because she showed her ass." That party confrontation made her feel that despite the similarities she shared with her school friends, she would always be different from them.

Everyone grows up and becomes socialized in a local environment, one where the natural inclination is to do exactly what other people your age are doing. However, your gender and skin color transmit messages to those around you that overwhelm your shared context with precoded expectations. In my formative years, I first experienced the clash between other peoples' expectations about who I was and what I should do, and who I really was as an individual. Twenty-plus years later, I shudder at the experiences I went through, except that without them I would not have been driven to investigate the problem further.

11. Metal Can Save Your Life (or at Least Your Sanity)

Like many preteens, I spent a lot of time hiding in my bedroom and listening to music. I would put on headphones and escape into a temporary fantasyland far away from reality. Playing air guitar, punching my pillows, and executing the occasional high kick, I fantasized about being a rock star and filled my head with healthier thoughts than those that were usually running around in there. Let's keep it real, shall we? Being a rock star is cool. Blocking out the misery that was primarily centered on killing people or hurting myself was the way to go.

Although I was plenty angry and frustrated, I didn't have the hardness—or the sociopathic or psychopathic tendencies—to walk into a school and shoot everyone in sight. I knew I harbored a potentially dangerous internal anger that was slowly bubbling to the surface. I also knew it was inappropriate to express my rage through words or violence.

I channeled my frustrations and counteracted my powerlessness by listening to the loudest, most aggressive music I could get my hands on, a habit I retain to this day. The music overrode my experiences of not belonging to either the white or black communities in my hometown. Consequently I came of age and reached adulthood obsessed with the issues surrounding racial identity and also heavy music.

As a black girl into metal, I had nobody with whom I could share my adoration for Rob Halford or my crush on the late Steve Clark from Def Leppard. While listening to music and perusing music magazines became a great form of escape, I always felt a bit of residual guilt. After all, black people—*real* black people—don't listen to metal.

I was dying to find other black female metal fans who were equally passionate about their ethnicity and their metal. I was always proud to be a black girl, but I struggled with people perceiving me as not being black enough. I traveled to as many concerts as I could afford, and I collected albums, concert T-shirts, and metal buttons. I encouraged others to use the music to create personal freedom to get them to acknowledge their feelings of anger and aggression. There was a lot of rage around me, and I knew it could be channeled into the positive energy that I found through metal.

If this sounds sunny in the context of heavy metal, consider that metal music can be heavy, dark, and ugly, but we fans see the beauty in the myriad of subgenres underneath the broader umbrella. I was drawn in by the comic-book visuals of Kiss after watching their made-for-TV movie *Kiss Meets the Phantom of the Park* in 1978. I loved their air of mystery. Later, I found more aggressive music with energy that compelled me to feel a bit more powerful in times when I didn't feel so powerful. All around the world, the reasons why we metal fans are passionate about our music remain very similar.

In 2008, the *College Student Journal* published the study "Effects of Listening to Heavy Metal Music on College Women." All of the participants were given a musical preference questionnaire to ensure that they did not have a liking for metal beforehand. These women, exposed to aggressive music for the first time, were found to be much more likely to grind their teeth! "Specifically, our findings suggest that heavy metal music elicits a physiological response in females, with significant differences between the silence and music conditions being focused at the masseter muscles during initial exposure. It is not clear why. . . ."

Among the factual findings, a main concern was that listening to metal could cause hearing damage, not a psychological breakdown. Since the lyrics of the songs used in the study were deemed indecipherable, the sponsors decided that the participants were reacting to the sound itself. To me, the physiological aspects are much less interesting than the psychological ones. I would love to know if metal listeners are more or less well balanced than the general public, and whether some personal trauma is necessary in order to have an affinity for the music.

In their findings, the researchers acknowledged that none of the eighteen participants were visible minorities, and they concluded that this should be investigated in a future study. That absence was frustrating. College students were used for convenience, which inherently limited the type of people surveyed. In my opinion, the study made some assumptions that because the women were all college students, and therefore affluent enough and intelligent enough to get into college, they were all relatively normal and could react objectively to the music.

A study isn't required to know that outsiders are commonly expected to be drawn toward metal, punk, and hardcore music. These are the people do not want to adhere to what their families and communities believe is the right way to behave. Sometimes music is that gateway. Coming to terms with her own unusual music choices liberated music journalist Keidra Chaney. "I didn't fit in," she says, "but I wasn't going to fit in anyway, so my loving metal was just another reason to be that weird chick. It wasn't a black identity issue, like me wanting to be like white folks because I grew up around only black folks. It wasn't an issue like I needed to choose. I just happened to be a weird black chick that happened to like weird music."

"It's extremely confusing as a black teenager," adds singer Camille Atkinson from Empire Beats. "Who knows who they are as a teenager? You are trying to assert your identity, but at the same time, you feel that you are being separated from your black identity."

Gravitating to the metal scene alleviated the pressure she felt coming out as a lesbian and helped shape her individuality. "When you are starting to redefine your identity, you do not always look at yourself as a descendant of a slave. You can look at it like you are the descendant of someone who had bought their freedom and is entitled to their own intellectual curiosity. We as young black women have to learn more about our actual history before we assume that we are all the same, that we all have the same denominators—because we don't."

"Frustration about not being respected. That's what metal is about," says Militia Vox, singer for Swear on Your Life and also the popular Judas Priest cover band Judas Priestess, "being the underdog and rising above. I think that on a subconscious level, the reason why I got into metal was because I went to all-white schools, private Catholic schools. Even though I was surrounded by white girls and a lot of them didn't listen to metal. They listened to R&B, pop, dance music and stuff in the '90s. Maybe because I'm black I have it in me to listen to rap, but more than that, it's in me to gravitate to whatever is extreme."

Depending on the sound, music can serve as a calming influence, a sexual aphrodisiac, or a massive boost of energy. Songs create an emotional bond between a sound and the listener. We might never meet the songwriter who reminds us of a recent heartbreak, or the performer who sang about the most important issues in our lives, but those songs stay with us. We identify with a particular song, or a sound, or an entire genre of music, and suddenly we feel less alone.

Nonfans mistake the rebellious exterior of heavy metal as a sullen, static thing, when in fact it is exhilarating to be reborn inside the music's storms. "People who listen to that genre of music don't question that," says Kudisan Kai, a vocal professor at Berklee College of Music who has recorded and toured with Elton John, Chaka Khan, Beck, and Mary J. Blige. "They just go, 'That's what I like,' and they just go do it. That's how they express it. If they don't like one band they will just listen to another. They don't analyze the exterior. I find a beautiful freedom in singing this heavy style of music. I have sung and studied a lot of music, but I have found that in this music, form allows that freedom and self-expression. And the audience is accepting of that kind of freedom; they love it because it is free."

"My way of getting through was being able to scream at the walls by listening to Mötley Crüe's *Shout at the Devil*," says Camille Atkinson. "There was some therapy in that. Putting on headphones and just listening to a group of people expressing their anger and allowing it to express how I was feeling. When I listen to some of the bands that are out there now, I don't necessarily understand what they are saying, but I understand the feeling of anger. There's nobody angrier than black teens in America. You're a teenager and your hormones are completely out of control—and then you're black."

"The bottom line is that music is a productive space for the release of anger, because it's not violent," adds music journalist and professor Devon Powers, who teaches communication at Philadelphia's Drexel College. "I think that anything that allows black women to have that space to express themselves and to not be perceived as violent or be the subject of either violence against yourself, or against another person, any release that you have is a good release. It makes me wonder why, if that potential for release is there, other people don't take advantage of it."

Speaking from experience, not enough black women take advantage of this potential release. For one thing, strife with friends and family often comes with the metal territory for anybody. Since the early 1970s, when Black Sabbath first emerged and metal became prevalent in North America, metal musicians and listeners have faced criticism about their chosen dress and perceived social dysfunction. Like a lot of black women, metal fans are often in the position of having to defend themselves against misinformation.

Especially for black women, who are often told from an early age that we have to be more aware of how others perceive us, how we appear in society is often more important that asserting our individuality. Following a punk or metal path can lead to an unhealthy amount of inner turmoil.

"Black women don't allow themselves to be liberated," says Laura Nicholls, who frequented Toronto's punk scene in the 1980s. "We do not allow ourselves to be free. It's not just listening to a diverse range of music that is perceived as being outside of black-centric musical styles—it's everything in our lives. Some of us do not allow ourselves to laugh loudly, to talk loudly, and we don't allow ourselves to be 'big,' because we don't want people to notice our behavior as an example of a negative racial stereotype—'Oh, she's acting that way because she's black.' The thing about black people is that we can be touched by anything because it seems as though we will never be able to satisfy anyone, so you might as well just be yourself. There is freedom in not following or adhering to the mold of what people expect you to be. You have to find what speaks to you."

Such resistance aside, the paths to discovery of metal were for a long time almost coincidental to begin with. The predominantly black hard rock and funk group Mother's Finest emerged from Atlanta with their self-titled debut in 1972. "Joyce Kennedy from Mother's Finest was one of the reasons why I got into rock music," says Kudisan Kai. "I had a boyfriend at the time that was into metal, and he was listening to a lot of different things, like early Judas Priest. He told me about Joyce's band. Everyone was listening to soul music, but metal was his thing. No one else was listening to metal, so I stood out like a sore thumb even mentioning that I was listening to such a thing."

During the 1980s, black women like metal and hardcore fans Erin Jackson and Monique Craft began to discover heavy metal through mass media and music videos. "I was different from a lot of the black kids that I know because I came from a very open-minded family in the sense that they were into so many different types of music," Jackson says. "My aunt exposed me at an early age to MTV's *Headbangers Ball* and I used to sit and just watch the guys with the tight pants and the high-topped sneakers and the big hair. I just thought it was awesome. When I was younger I was always the oddball, because I was always into rock music. I grew up in Newark, New Jersey, and all the kids at school were into gangsta rap. They would be like, 'You're not white. You should be listening to this group.'"

In the 1990s, black families in urban areas were deciding that city living wasn't the best atmosphere to raise families. Higher incomes made relocating to less ethnically diverse communities or to the suburbs possible. There seemed to be more room to grow and live in safer communities. All of a sudden there were many more children like me who went to schools where they were the minority, exploring music and culture that would seem alien back in their previous neighborhoods.

Craft grew up in a white environment in Connecticut. "I went to a private school where there was only me and another black kid, and she wasn't even black; she was Dominican. In high school, I got beaten up because I was wearing jeans and an oversize black T-shirt. Finally one day, a girl sat me down and said, 'Look, you might want to rethink how you dress here, because it's weird to them and it's going to be even weirder if you dress that way and you're the only black kid.' I'm sure that if there were more black girls in the scene, people wouldn't be so weirded out. I wish I could let other girls know that it's okay, that there are more people like us and they aren't unicorns."

Like me, Karma Elise, music journalist and cofounder of FourteenG. net, was first introduced to metal through Kiss. "I didn't really get into metal until I was fourteen," she says. "But I also saw the trend among my friends who were into R&B music who refused to even go down that road of finding something else that they possibly could like, because their parents weren't into it. Just because your parents weren't into it doesn't mean that you can't like it. Because it's something out of your normal pool, people tend to turn their backs on it, and it's a shame, because it's something that you are really missing out on."

Urith Myree, bassist for New Jersey's Dormitory Effect, did grow up in a black neighborhood, and her father was a member of the Black Panther

Party. However, he turned her onto the diverse underground music that his friends favored, and thus she heard hard rock for the first time at home. "I grew up in an age when there really wasn't a separation in music," she says. "People listened to everything, but musicians had to really know how to play. It didn't matter what you looked like."

Out in the world, she found she had to fight to remain steadfast in her love for hard rock and later metal. Again there was resistance. "Once you start liking hard rock music, and you have that 'gene' in you, you start off with a little bit of Led Zeppelin, Sabbath, you just progress from there," she says. "Then it was Iron Maiden and then it became the heavier stuff, and then it was like, 'Whoa, what is this? Who are these screaming white guys? Why do you like this stuff?' It's tough to explain, but it speaks to me. It took my friends and some family members a while to understand why it appealed to me, but they eventually got to the point when it became, 'Whatever.'"

"Part of the problem in black communities is that our diverse experiences are not recognized," says Pisso, a former skinhead involved in the punk and hardcore scene. "I didn't grow up in the hood or the projects. At the time I got into punk, I was living in an Orthodox Jewish neighborhood on the north side of Chicago. But that doesn't make my experiences better or worse than anyone else's. When I was in seventh grade I went to a new school, so my clothes weren't the most fashionable or cool, and the kids would tease me about that. When I got into punk, that wasn't an issue at all—what your family background is, and if you were wearing older clothes, the better. I didn't have to feel ashamed about not having money.

"I just wish that black people would realize that each time you meet a black person, their experiences are individual and unique. Some people who have met me for the first time automatically assume that I'm dissing my hood or I'm not being 'real.' They have no idea of where I grew up, my values, or my cultural background. They are expecting an authenticity from me that I can't even give them."

I do not think punk and metal are all about anger for black women. Otherwise a myriad of metal, hardcore, and punk fans would have abandoned their fandom after surviving their troubled teenage years. Adults everywhere use angry music to calm down, to convert negative energy into positivity, and to retain a sense of control in a world where it can be stripped away at the turn of a dime.

As a young adult entering the workforce, I felt that my opinions were not seen as valid when they differed from the experiences of my nonblack coworkers. I did not act matronly like Clair Huxtable, and I was not as "hood" as Salt-N-Pepa, so who exactly was I? I do not think that my employers judged me by my personality or my smarts, but according to their own prejudices. A male coworker once said to me, "So you're twenty-two and you don't have any kids? I thought you people had lots of kids." Another coworker told a white coworker whom I was dating not to sleep with me, because "black women carry syphilis."

Whenever I questioned behavior like this, I heard "You should be lucky that you have this job . . ." or apartment . . . or salary. I could feel palpable pressure to be seen but not heard—and then only if they needed to see me at all.

Maybe the reserved social manners of Canada kept a tighter lid on anger, frustration—and racial ignorance. "Canada is a predominantly white society. Very white, culturally," says Laura Nichols. "I'm a fighter, so when I was at a punk show, I'd be very provocative. I feel that there is a lot of power in being a black woman, because young white guys are probably the most insecure people in the world. I was just as fucked up inside as the next person, but I knew how to intimidate people. You had to learn how to navigate in a white society, and I learned that in order to navigate, I had to intimidate."

As a young adult, I lived in a city with more black people. I regularly danced to house music and hip hop at after-hours clubs, but I still gravitated toward heavier sounds. Now that I was little bit older, the political messages of some bands pulled at my head as much as the aggression pulled at my heart. "Metal definitely pulled me up as a kid," says Camille Atkinson. "There was one band in particular that stood out to me, Anthrax. They have a song called 'Schism,' and I swear they had all taken sociology classes! The song was about how racism, fascism, and all that was total bullshit. Then there's Queensrÿche's *Operation: Mindcrime*, which was brilliant commentary! The innovative correlation between the aggressiveness and the beauty was perfect in talking about social issues.

"As a thirteen-year-old who wanted to get out of church, I really needed to hear that," she continues. "'No, Mom, the church is evil! You should hear what they did to Sister Mary!' I thought they were lying, and I was coming out as a lesbian, and as a Catholic, the guilt that goes along with that is incredible. It was very personal for me. You have people on both sides of your life, your family life and your peers, telling you that you are not black enough because you listen to this music. So you *do* question yourself. What ends up happening is that you create for yourself an identity of what a black person *should* be."

Atkinson discovered that as an adult she had the power to bring together isolated black rock fans. "I once played at a black club that was actually a rock venue, and I felt that I was coming home, you know? There were black folks with long dreadlocks and these Metallica T-shirts. It was the first time that I thought, 'I can bang my head in this room and no one is going to think I'm a freak.' I have to say that from only being in a white rock environment, there was a part of me that felt relieved. It was the only time I wasn't the only black person there! There's a part of me that wants white people to know what it feels like to be the only minority in the room. It was a nice change of pace, and it made me feel that the world is getting bigger."

After the show, she communed with the listeners, a powerful experience. "They were like, 'Yeah, this is our music!' Besides the fact that they all lived in probably the most culturally and ethnically diverse city in the world, New York, they all seemed excited to meet each other at that particular club, knowing without openly admitting that their passion for nonblack-oriented music made them unique."

⚡

Many black women make a soft landing in outsider music by gravitating toward punk and hardcore. Gaining popularity in 1975, punk initially served as an example of the ethnic cleansing of rock music, marked by disdain for blues-tinged rock music. "It's more about attitude and speed. You can have a whole song in thirty seconds and it's all about aggression," says LaRonda Davis, president of the Black Rock Coalition, or BRC. "You can't understand the words and there is no melody to speak of, versus metal, which is just heavy, heavy noise."

Davis mentions that the punk scene in New York, which in the '80s was primarily an all-white scene, wasn't so welcoming to blacks. "The Knives was this gang that was made up of black and Latino members. They would protect kids at shows that might get their asses kicked because of the white skinheads there. But it was really about fighting—you had to fight to earn your way in to see the music, which was crazy."

"For me, I got into punk after I got into metal, and usually it's the other way around," adds Earl Douglas, executive director of the BRC. "I had my first punk experience in sophomore year in high school, but metal told more of a story. The leather jacket, the jeans had a more relatable look— everybody wears jeans and everyone wore leather to a certain degree. Metal was more . . . It was slower. It meant more."

The early-'80s hardcore and punk scene was the only musical forum where black youth could talk about politics. Ronald Reagan served two terms as president of the United States, and many felt social and politically repressed and were trying to find avenues to tell the world how angry they were. For black women, punk, just like the blues, was a music in which they could temporarily eschew the societal constraints that had been imposed by their families and communities.

Compared to metal, the hardcore and punk scenes have always included more black faces. The subject matter directly addresses political issues that draw the attention of socially, politically, and economically marginalized groups. As displayed by the underground popularity of such bands as Bad Brains and 24-7 Spyz, the cross-pollination between punk and Caribbean in the form of ska and reggae music might have made punk slightly more palatable for black folks.

Singers X-Ray Spex's Poly Styrene and Jingo de Lunch's Yvonne Ducksworth are only two of the black women fronting punk bands. "I found a connection to punk music because when they talked about their musical forefathers, they were talking about black people," says Laura Nicholls. "Bands like the Jam—that was '60s, '70s soul right there. They were talking about things politically that I agreed with. That attracted me, not just because the music made me feel good, which it did, but it was the lyrics that described the political and social issues at the time. Art is liberating, and I think that you will always find things to connect with."

"What ended up bringing me into hardcore was just really coming to a historical cultural awareness as a young black person in America," says Tamar-kali. "When I was becoming politically aware, it was a progression, because at first, I was into new wave and alternative music, as I was more melancholy. When I became more politically aware, I was getting frustrated and indignant about the system, and there was a lot of information in punk music at that time and the politics involved with the Dead Kennedys and other punk bands."

"I wanted to be special, to be different—be the only one and be different from what they thought black people were about," says Nicholls. "There was a lot of insecurity and fucked-up things surrounding what I did at that time. But my interest was genuine and the music did speak to me. There was also a bit of perverseness there, like, 'I'm not going to do what you want me to do or what you think I should be doing.' In a way, I figured that my life as a black person in Canada was so different, why not? It's liberating because it leaves you open to different things, but in a way, you are constantly putting yourself in situations where you are always the only one."

Yet the '80s punk scene in New York, especially with the skinheads, wasn't so welcoming at first. "I grew up in the '80s, when there were more metal bands on MTV than punk bands," says the BRC's Davis. "Everything was about metal, watered-down metal, cheesy metal. There were punk videos that played during one segment, and that was it."

Ironically, the rap world was often more keen on metal than on punk. "I think metal was a lot more tolerable," adds Douglas. "Early Run-DMC had metal guitars on their album. The B-boys would say, 'That is hot.' Punk was more about speed and aggression and we were like, 'We just want to sit back and listen to a song instead of worrying about getting into a fight.' I think metal was a lot more friendly, slightly more inviting than punk was, where you had to be initiated."

Compared to a leap into the punk scene, venturing into the tougher hard rock and heavy metal crowd can be daunting, not only because of the common assumptions that with heavy and rough music come heavy and rough people. Musicians also have to step up their game, as metal puts more emphasis on musical proficiency than hardcore and punk. But when questioned about their highs, black woman champion the benefits of metal in glowing refrains.

For concert photographer Erika Kristen, who cofounded FourteenG. net, involvement in the DIY realm of metal allowed her develop her zeal for music into an actual career in the metal music industry. "As I grew older," she says, "I wouldn't tell people. My music preference was not usually discussed, but if it did come up that I was into the metal music scene, then I would take the Obama way about it. I would ignore the puzzled stares and negative comments. It just is. Accept it or not, I don't give a fuck. It's a very metal thing about being metal. You either like it or you don't.

"I was born into a group of very arrogant bastards, so they instilled in me that you should never put your head down in any situation you go into," she continues. "I used to work for this large media company on Michigan Avenue in Chicago, and I would walk into a place just like I owned it. Believe in your merit, not the color of your skin, as to whether you can do something or not do something. And I have basked in that belief ever since I was a kid."

"Overall, I think that you have to act like racism and sexism don't exist when you are involved in the metal scene," says Dallas Coyle, a founding guitarist of God Forbid. "A racist, someone who hates black people, will talk to a black person like he is one of his best friends. And then he will say, 'He's one of the good ones.' It happens all the time, and not just about black people and whites. It's just human nature. But you can't let it exist for you, because if it can exist for you, then it does for everyone else, and people will sense that you are always looking around and being nervous."

Alexis Brown of Straight Line Stitch veered from a singing career in black-centric music to extreme metal. "It's funny because my aunt used to tell me all the time that I should be doing something other than R&B music," she says. "That used to make me so mad, because at the time I was like, 'No, I'm a black girl, I *should* be doing R&B.'" She laughs. "I ended up falling in love with the metal genre and this is my career now. I'm seeing a lot more girls coming out to shows. It is amazing. I have young girls coming up to me and saying they are so excited to see me out there representing the black female community. They get ridiculed at school because they are really into Suicide Silence. [When they wear] our T-shirts, the other black kids make fun of them. You just gotta be you, and be more of a leader and not a follower. I'm not a leader or anything; I'm just trying to be me."

In 2008, Kudisan Kai organized a three-day symposium titled "Black Women in Rock" at the Berklee College of Music in Boston, where she is a professor in the voice department. That fall, vocalist Nona Hendryx, Mother's Finest singer Joyce Kennedy, drummers Cindy Blackman and Terri Lyne Carrington, singer-songwriter Siedah Garrett, and bassist Meshell Ndegeocello led panel discussions, moderated workshops, and performed for students and the general public. "One of the issues that I have had singing other types of music is that there was this criterion that I always had to follow," Kai admits. "I had to have the 'hot riff' for the R&B stuff, or there was just always something where I felt I was always putting myself and what I wanted to do aside."

Her colleagues at the esteemed music school responded to the first-ever symposium of its kind with total surprise. "Eventually I got a good response from black faculty members," she says, "but initially, they were shocked. 'Why are you doing this?' Their mouths flew open, and while I think they were happy about it, they still didn't know what to do with it. I think that it's leftover baggage from the thought that rock music is beneath black people, that we had overcome rock 'n' roll when we integrated.

"Rock and metal music allows you to be who you want to be, [to] stand behind it, scream it out loud, and understand that it's okay to be angry," she affirms. "Women sometimes don't feel that it's okay to be angry. I had to learn, and that was a major thing for me. It's okay to express who you are, and there is nothing wrong with it, and there is no criterion around it. It's one of the few places as a black woman that you get an opportunity to be free, be who you are without any questions, without caring. [That's how it] is when I am on that stage, doing that kind of music."

Kristen urges black metalheads to stand up for the metal scene. "This is how ignorance is perpetuated," she says. "We have to learn how to speak up against it. Even if it is to our friends, our family members. If they love you or care about you in any capacity, they will help to build your character and [respect] what you believe in, not try and tear it down and make a mockery of it."

III. I'm Here Because We Started It!

WHEN WE FACE SOCIAL AND POLITICAL TURMOIL, black folks are commonly told to look to the past for answers. The legacies of Martin Luther King and Rosa Parks are held up as examples of how we should handle struggle, using logical reasoning and measured, intelligent responses to adversity. For those whose family lineage dates back to the slave era, parents and grandparents retell the experiences of their ancestors, reminding their offspring of family members who had it a hell of a lot worse: "Be strong. That is the only way you are going to get through life."

Music is not only for enjoyment. We derive too much pleasure, pain, and education from the music that we listen to every day to dismiss it as simply entertainment. For black populations in Western civilization, music has provided a voice in times when their own were silenced. Music also transmitted important messages that were integral to survival—and still functions in that role today, in language far more blatant than the coded slave-era field hollers and shouts.

I was pleased and relieved that the women I interviewed for *What Are You Doing Here?* often made a correlation between their heritage and the nuances within heavy metal, hardcore, and punk music that affects us so profoundly. After all, if the blues, a black-originated sound, served as the musical and spiritual foundation of metal, hardcore, and punk, why is there so much resistance among black people to listening to it?

Urith Myree talks about growing up in the black community. "If you showed up with a denim jacket with a skull on the back, like the thrash metal style, people would stop you and go, 'What's that?' If I had an Iron Maiden Eddie logo badge, it was like, 'What's that and why do you have that on your jacket? Why do you listen to that type of music?' I don't recall anyone being really hostile about it, but there was a lot of curiosity. I just liked the music. I didn't like the restrictions of what I could listen to. I had white guys come up and say to their friends, 'Oh, look at that black chick. That's just not something that you see.' And I was like, 'Sorry, this is as much my music as it is yours. If it weren't for the blues people that influenced the British bands, you wouldn't have Black Sabbath. I have just as much claim to the music as you do.'"

In metal, hardcore, and punk, the visual aesthetics of music are historically influenced by the long and Mohawk haircuts of Native American culture and the vibrant face paint and body piercing of African tribes. "Those first extreme looks in the punk scene, they were doing it in England," says singer Tamar-kali, who sang for Funkface and Song of Seven. "I just found that really ironic because Britain is that O.G., imperialist type of nation. It is interesting that the aesthetic that they were going for was the aesthetic that their grandfathers were colonizing. I don't know if it was intentional or not, but they dyed their hair all these colors—and ended up looking like the natives of a lot of these countries that Britain colonized."

"A lot of African music is noise," says Monique Craft, who studied African tribes as a part of establishing her own black identity. "If you throw some double bass and some gnarly guitar behind it, it sounds exactly like metal, but it's really African tribe music. So when people start questioning my musical tastes and my tattoos, I respond with something along the lines of 'Well, there is this African tribe called the Masai, and they look a lot like me, but I'm wearing clothes.'"

"Those images, whatever they want to call it—primordial, primitive," says Tamar-kali, "you can see how they adorned themselves in these ways and so these kids were contemporizing it and putting their own spin on it. That look thing that Bow Wow Wow put together—they even called that style 'tribal.' It's clear that they were trying to look like 'savages' or whatever."

⚡

As a kid, I was familiar with only two women blues singers: Billie Holiday and Bessie Smith. Holiday was a beautiful black woman who sang "Strange Fruit," a harrowing song about watching the aftermath of a group lynching in the South. The songwriter Abel Meeropol originally published the words as a poem. The song had been sung by others before Holiday recorded it in 1939, but her interpretation, often sung a cappella during live performances, resonated with the public. Her delivery and knack for finding the nuances in the song reveal truth through music, as the various live performances of the song more than prove.

In North Carolina in July 1927, Bessie Smith faced down a group of Ku Klux Klan members as they attempted to shut down her performance on a makeshift stage inside a tent. When she was informed that the Klan were outside trying to pull out the pegs that kept the tent upright, she immediately went out to confront them. Standing before them, she clenched her fists and threatened to set the entire audience upon them if they didn't leave.

Both Holiday and Smith had tragic lives. Raped at age eleven, Holiday had a long history of alcohol and drug abuse. Smith struggled with abusive men and personal demons. Though her lyrics were filled with tales of lost loves and no-good men, she also sang openly about her sexual needs and desires. Both women helped usher in a new model of black female performer—more sexual in appearance and onstage mannerisms, more vocal, independent, and realistic. They were the first to show many people of their eras, especially white audiences, that black women were just as sexually aware and confident as their white counterparts. In the blues era, such self-assured black female performers provided a small glimpse into all the different layers of their complex personalities. They eventually assisted with the slow decline of the barriers of sexism and racism within the larger society—but it didn't come easy.

Despite the historical importance of female blues singers to American music, those important models for independence and confidence didn't carry into the modern age. With each generation came a push-and-pull of whether black female performers actually served as positive role models or represented a hypersexualized image that black communities would soon rather forget.

Billie Holiday's emotional connection to the subject matter of "Strange Fruit" and Bessie Smith's life story were integral for me discovering the roots that connected blues music and hard rock music, and seem to hold some key to a possible role for black women in heavy metal. The blues was greatly influential in the birth of rock 'n' roll. The appeal seemed universal, and over time people traded in light melodies in favor of a heavier sound. Throughout rock history, that bit of rhythmic aggression is universal.

Pain and perseverance are common themes in blues music and in metal, hardcore, and punk. During the era of slavery in North America, it was beneficial for those involved in the transactions of buying, selling, and maintaining African slaves to paint them all as having the same intellectual, emotional, and physical traits. This streamlined the product, made it more easily controllable, and allowed them and to rationalize their own behavior: The more emotionally removed they were from slaves, the easier it was to enslave them. Among slaves, codes of conduct were developed, both out of necessity and to help maintain humanity and cultural traditions in an era where the stripping of these was monetarily beneficial.

While other ethno-cultural groups have codes of behavior and cultural scripts, for North American slaves following the codes could determine whether they lived or died. Work songs, field hollers, shouts, chants, and dance communicated these codes and fostered cultural and emotional bonds to past lives in Africa or the Caribbean. Ironically, according to Darrell M. McNeill's essay "Rock, Racism, and Retailing 101: A Blueprint for Cultural Theft," slave owners actually preferred the slaves to sing, shout, and dance.

A willingness to perform when ordered seemed to show that slaves were submissive, ignorant, and easily controlled. The slave owners didn't glean that the jigs the slaves were performing, along with their field hollers, were methods to transmit important messages and were coded to avoid detection. Ultimately, the more the slaves entertained their owners, the longer the slaves stayed alive.

After the slave era, blues music, inspired by those songs sung in the fields of the plantations, and gospel music created an environment where black men and women could assert their individuality, as their personalities normally had to be tucked away as they toiled as domestics and laborers. Played in shabby, makeshift bars in rural areas, the music slowly got the attention of white record producers and was transmitted to the general public.

With the growing popularity of this new musical hybrid came criticism. "Blues music is the devil's music" was a common refrain from churchgoing black folks, as popularity among white listeners grew. Negro spirituals were popular because of their positive, inspirational vocals. Those songs were inspired by the Bible, and many felt that blues music bastardized them. "When people say that the blues is [the] devil's music, it's because they are taking something holy from gospel, used for worship, and using it for something less holy," explains Camille Atkinson.

For Smith and other black female blues singers of the 1920s, '30s, and '40s, singing about their lives, loves, and struggles was the only way that they could safely express sexual longing, romantic love, jealousy, and depression. Otherwise, black female perspectives were generally ignored at the time. These women brought a glimmer of hope for black female listeners, as the emotional conflicts they expressed were common, yet suppressed.

The arrival of black female blues guitarists like Little Laura Dukes and Memphis Minnie in the 1930s and 1940s created a strong image for black women who dared to master what was considered a "male" musical instrument. They also helped popularize the first stirrings of rock 'n' roll. In that time period, a number of black women blues musicians chose to forge their own paths and break from codes of conduct imposed within black communities. Basically, they put their freedom of expression above their personal security, and couldn't have cared less about staying on the good side of the whites.

Cynthia Dagnal-Myron, a former music journalist for the *Chicago Sun-Times* and *Creem*, believes that the blues era was the beginning of a legacy of assertive black female performers. "These women would twist [the negative stereotypes about black women] around and throw it in the face of the audience. There were blues women who were not attractive at all, sang as hard as men, and drank as hard as the men, and it had nothing to do with who they were as women. There's a precedent to that, but if you were to act like that today, you would have to be willing to take the anger from the audience."

Born in 1926, blues singer Big Mama Thornton is a good example of the importance of black women in the blues era—and of the differences in record sales depending on who was singing the song. Her 1952 hit single "Hound Dog" was number one on the *Billboard* R&B charts for seven weeks, yet she reportedly never received the profits of the almost two million copies sold of the single. Elvis Presley recorded his version in 1956 and went on to become a superstar. Thornton wrote and recorded the song "Ball and Chain," which also later became a huge hit for a white singer, Janis Joplin, in the 1960s.

When more whites became interested in going to blues and jazz clubs, some of the only places blacks could enjoy themselves away from the critical eyes of whites, blacks found they could no longer relax. Whites brought money, which became the main focus. Behavior that would not promote racial stereotypes was encouraged, though the barroom ethics of drinking, fighting, and fucking couldn't really be repressed. When hedonistic behavior occasionally spilled out of the juke joints and into the real world, black people got nervous. What they did on a Saturday night translated into how they were treated at work, or how their children interacted with kids outside of their communities.

Maureen Mahon, the author of *Right to Rock: The Black Rock Coalition and the Cultural Politics of Race* and a professor at New York University, explains the transition from the blues era to rock 'n' roll and the popularity of some of the earliest black rock artists. "I think what happened in the 1960s, or even in the 1950s, is that rock 'n' roll was pretty interracial in terms of audience and performers. As more and more white people became involved, the music changed, and black people followed other types of music."

"As more white people became attracted to rock 'n' roll, black people started to construct it as 'This is something for them, this isn't for us,'" she explains. "There were always black people participating and present, but they started to be outnumbered."

The early black rock 'n' roll musicians were being squeezed out of the scene, anyway. Not only did white civic leaders make their hostility toward black rockers known, so did middle-class black communities who wanted to put the low-down and dirty music and culture behind them. "[Many black Americans] were against the shouting and the screaming and felt that the blues was setting the black race back," explains Kudisan Kai. "They thought that we were above that, that 'we had gotten past that, that we were integrated now.'" Black musicians, whose talent was still appreciated, were pushed to the back, not exactly invisible but less visible. Many found themselves working as backup musicians for white musicians.

Rock 'n' roll, blues, and jazz albums were banned in many black homes. Many families felt that the music was unsuitable—that it was sacrilegious and conveyed messages that were too personal and too sexual. More importantly, the sexual desire, emotional woes, and relationship issues that the female blues singers detailed in their lyrics signified a freedom from male oppression, which threatened the sanctity of the black nuclear household.

"I think that if you want to stereotype you could ask, What music qualities do black people value?" adds Maureen Mahon. "Something in terms of the voice capacity, a centrality of the voice in performance which kind of exists in rock, but people may not hear the type of singing that rock singers do as meeting a standard in which they would say, 'This is quality music' or 'This is good.' People can do very well in traditional rock without singing well in a traditional sense. Jimi Hendrix is a good example, as I would say that he had a great voice but he was afraid to sing. He thought that he couldn't sing well, according to the terms of what a typical black member of the black community like the one he came out of would have expected."

"When you had black people doing rock music, black people didn't know what to do," says writer Cynthia Dagnal-Myron. "It's loud, it's raunchy, and it's bluesy. It's a black person emulating a white person trying to do a black person. They don't know what to do with that. It came out with R&B music and you either fell into that or you didn't. And they maintain that story until this day. They maintain that separation."

Black women were literally pushed to the rear of the stage, notably as backup singers, injecting a soulful sound popularized in the 1970s by Pink Floyd, Steely Dan, and the Rolling Stones, all bands greatly influenced by blues music. Despite their integral contribution to the overall sounds of the bands they supported and perhaps injecting a bit of soulful credibility to their songs and their reputations, black female backup singers were used as decorative wallpaper, a kind of exotic secret ingredient.

Singer Venetta Fields recounted her experience as a backup singer for Humble Pie and the Blackberries in the late '60s and '70s in Kandia Crazy Horse's book *Rip It Up*. "Every time we opened our mouths and sang or made up a part and sang it, the crowd would get so excited. That was the time when every act had to have three black American singers in the band. They wanted to feel and hear the blackness. They would pay anything to get it or experience it." She goes on to say that she didn't really realize until much later the significance that her group the Blackberries had in paving the way for other female musical acts.

Black female singers of that era had a difficult time. Funk music, a blend of soul, jazz, rock, and R&B music, was a healthy compromise between black music and white-oriented rock 'n' roll. The music was black, but the performers dressed and acted more seductively than was comfortable for middle-class black Americans. "When I was young, you had the Supremes, you had blues people, and you had Chaka Khan," says Dagnal-Myron. "People were like, 'What is that?' She sold a certain kind of sexuality, but it wasn't a sexuality that black men liked. But she had that voice; otherwise I don't know where she would have gone. She sang R&B and funk, but her look—that was a danger for black women at that time. It turned people on their heads, they didn't know whether to respect her or not."

Tina Turner was able to transcend the Ike and Tina Turner Revue and forge a highly successful career performing radio-friendly rock 'n' roll. Her success as a black rock singer might be an anomaly, but her first three solo albums all flopped: the cheesy *Tina Turns the Country On,* a collection of country rock covers; 1975's *Acid Queen*; and 1978's *Rough,* which showcased Turner's love for rock 'n' roll. She didn't shine on her own until she decided to sing adult contemporary and R&B music that was more in line with her being a middle-aged black woman in America. She reigned as a tough rock singer onstage in blond shock wigs, revealing miniskirts, low-cut tops, and stiletto heels, but marketers didn't know how to market her.

Turner's 1983 remake of Al Green's "Lets Stay Together" hit the charts in England and got her noticed. The single didn't reach the American charts until the next year, while she waited for an American record deal. Her subsequent single "What's Love Got to Do With It?" became one of her most successful songs, but initially only eleven radio stations put it on regular rotation. Her album *Private Dancer* eventually sold eleven million records worldwide, but that road to stardom began overseas. The Germans, the French, and the Brazilians loved her. In the mid-1980s she moved permanently to Europe.

Less well-known black female rock artists include singer Betty Davis, whose 1973 debut, *Betty Davis*, predated Turner's rock career and was the first of four she released before fading into obscurity in the late 1970s. While Davis might have not produced the quintessential rock sound, her edgy lyrics and hypersexual delivery were straight-up rock 'n' roll, giving male counterparts like Robert Plant and Mick Jagger a run for their money in the sexuality department.

Both Turner and Davis are strikingly beautiful. During their heyday, onstage, their long legs were prominently displayed in short skirts and fuck-me pumps; low necklines revealed impressive cleavage. A beautiful, young, fashionable black woman in the '70s, Davis sported an impressive Afro. That dress and attitude were provocative and, for some, too much.

According to Vivien Goldman's essay "Blues for Betty Davis's Smile: The Betty Davis Lacuna," religious groups banned some of Davis's shows. "Playing the savage beast card had become part of Betty's MO by now; though really, she hadn't been all that animal or even outrageously wild. She just sang vibrantly about what many a female feels on a Friday night, and did, exuberantly, what came naturally, her lust for life unrestrained by the girdle of anyone's expectations." Just as they didn't care for Jimi Hendrix, who was at the height of his career at the same time that Davis was married to jazz legend Miles Davis, the black community was not too fond of her musical selection or her attitude.

Perhaps Davis was too outspoken, perpetrating an image that many black people, especially women in the audience, didn't appreciate. At that time, black female rock singers were caught between a rock and a hard place. They had to project an attractive and fashionable image that was contemporary but not too risqué for black audiences, yet also appealing enough to gain and maintain the attention of white audiences. If that meant dipping their toes into sexual stereotypes in order to gain the interest of white audiences, so be it—but it was difficult to do two things at once.

"A lot of it is the way Americans understand who we are, and for black and white Americans, part of understanding who is in what category has to do with opposition to the other category, " says Mahon. "[Often] how black culture gets presented or how black people understand themselves is in contrast to white people or white culture, and vice versa. For white people, their awareness may not be as key, because they do not have to think about identity in the same way, because they are not the minority population."

When the black power movement took hold in the 1970s, black Americans attempted more and more to separate themselves from popular culture and music. "There is this desire to keep everything separate," says Mahon. "I think that the overarching thing for Americans is this separation that people are so insistent on, because it really doesn't exist. There is so much mixing that it is important to insist on a separation in order to make sense of things. It made it really hard for it to make sense to be interested in rock 'n' roll, if you were a black person, according to the logic of black cultural nationalism."

This divide was unfortunate, and, as a black woman heavy metal fan I can definitely feel the effects today. "This whole 'race' construct is just crazy if you look at how music had to jump from basically being Irish and Native American drum-inspired music," adds Camille Atkinson. "If it wasn't for all these different strange encounters between the different racial groups, we wouldn't have rock music the way it is. And it only grows because it goes through these different patterns."

Despite the black nationalism of the Black Panther movement that encouraged black Americans to turn their attention to black-centric culture, some members were also involved in the burgeoning hard rock and metal scene. Interestingly enough, the rise of black power coincided with what is commonly deemed the first North American heavy metal single, Blue Cheer's 1968 cover of "Summertime Blues." The San Francisco trio pushed Eddie Cochran's rock 'n' roll hit into oblivion with unthinkable amounts of distortion, feedback, loudness, and sheer power. Jimi Hendrix's "Purple Haze," released in 1967, is another contender, as is even the Kinks' 1964 hit "You Really Got Me," with its key power riff. These elements reached a breaking point in 1970 with what is widely considered the first authentic heavy metal album, Black Sabbath's self-titled debut.

Whether you define heavy metal by its musical sound, or by the symbolism and lyrics, heavy metal originated from several different sources. According to Robert Walser, author of *Running with the Devil: Power, Gender and Madness in Heavy Metal*, the roots of metal can be traced back as far as bluesmen Robert Johnson and Howlin' Wolf. Walser suggests that Led Zeppelin singer Robert Plant borrowed his signature vocal style from soul singer James Brown. "The debt of heavy metal to African-American music making," he writes, "has vanished from most accounts of the genre, just as black history has been suppressed in every other field."

"When you look back at the old-school bands, in particular Led Zeppelin and the Doors, they started off as blues bands," adds journalist Sameerah Blue, founder of the blog *Ecto Mag*. "They wanted to play blue-eyed soul, that's what they wanted to be. Even if you listen to interviews with Robert Plant now and he talks about his influences, he very seldom ever mentions rock bands—he's always talking about blues bands and blues singers. For some reason, no one could ever buy them as blues bands, so they developed their own kind of variation."

"With rock, it seems like ever since it took off in popularity and it got occupied by a white audience, it was disconnected from the black community," says Pisso, a black former skinhead from Chicago. "Through out the years, there have always been black musicians in the scene, so I don't understand why there is this resistance. In terms of the culture of rock, punk, and metal, I always thought what bothered my mom was the presumed lifestyle that went along with it: Wearing wear ripped-up stuff, dirty clothes from the thrift store. You wear your hair crazy, and that was just not the image that she wanted to present to the world of her daughter. She would have been much happier if I had been listening to R&B or something a little tamer."

But was R&B tamer? "It's not wholesome," she laughs. "All the half-naked girls are doing speed and stuff like that. I don't understand why rock has this negative image and hip hop or even R&B are supposed to be better. But it could also just be a fear of difference, a fear of standing out. If everybody listens to a couple of artists but your child is listening to something else, you are going to worry that they are not going to fit in, be integrated."

Being confounded by black women with strong images is nothing new. "Men have been historically intimidated by intense women, women who have intense personalities and behaviors," adds metal singer Militia Vox. "I've been labeled a man hater in the rock scene. They want their females to be easily digestible. You can't be too strong. If I was going to sell out like that I would have done it already."

According to Trey Ellis's 1989 article "The New Black Aesthetic" in the journal *Callaloo*, the "post-black" mid-'80s welcomed a new generation of musicians. Black rock, punk, and metal bands like Living Colour, Fishbone, 24-7 Spyz, Bad Brains, Mother's Finest, and the Family Stand chose to eschew the societal constraints that had formed around blacks in the wake of the post–civil rights era, during the hippie liberation (where white folks could get away with being unemployed ne'er-do-wells but black folks just got locked up) of the '70s and the socially repressive eight years that Ronald Reagan was president of the United States, and simply *live*. They wanted to openly acknowledge the music that surrounded them, which they could hear on a hot summer's evening coming from their white or Hispanic neighbors' apartments in Bedford-Stuyvesant or the South Side of Chicago, or from the records they snuck home and hid under their beds. For the first time, angry, confrontational lyrics were not hidden under a soft, sensual voice and beautiful melodies, à la Marvin Gaye's "What's Going On," but were matched with angry, aggressive music.

These were black musicians who, despite emerging during the same era as rap, decided to reclaim the music that their forefathers had created. They took back the blues and chose to appreciate jazz, which had been regulated as music for the bourgeois, and added a rock 'n' roll twist. Some folks like myself, who were lucky enough to get cable TV just in time to watch *Soul in the City*, a one-hour music video program on Toronto's MuchMusic video station that was dedicated to airing black-oriented alternative music, thought they had died and gone to heaven. Rock, punk, and metal music by black musicians! It seemed like the best of both worlds.

"In terms of the sound of the music," says Maureen Mahon, "something that you will often hear from black people who don't listen to rock 'n' roll and aren't steeped in rock culture is that it's so loud [and] there's the focus on the guitar, which is an instrument that fell out of favor in black communities by the early 1960s. It was always there but it wasn't the focal point. Suddenly you have a genre of music where the guitar is the focal point; the guitar solo—a *loud* guitar solo—became important in the music. And then there is the issue of singing or vocal quality."

"We started rock," says Camille Atkinson. "Robert Johnson was rock, that was the first rock it ever was, and you could say that it is our right to sing it more than anyone else. The truth of the matter is that it's a mélange. It's about everybody acknowledging the fact that it comes from all these different roots, and saying, 'Okay, it *is* black music.' People just never really acknowledge it, but it is."

The Rolling Stones' Mick Jagger shelled out the money and muscle to help Living Colour record their early demos. Preceding Living Colour as one of the first black hard rock/metal bands to be represented by a major label was Mother's Finest. On the band's 1976 self-titled debut, they acknowledged their frustration with the attitude they were getting from black communities about their music with the song "Niggizz Can't Sing

Rock 'n' Roll." In 1992, Mother's Finest released *Black Radio Won't Play This Record*, a metal album with heavy doses of soul and funk that matched the Atlanta-based band's frustration over continuously being ignored by black media and radio outlets.

In 1985, a group of New York–based black rock musicians and fans banded together and created the Black Rock Coalition, or BRC. In an interview in the BRC's newsletter, *Progressive Forum*, on the coalition's fifteenth anniversary in 2000, Greg Tate explained why the organization was founded. "We really started out as a way to air out certain gripes that people had about the 'glass ceiling' in music for black musicians. Particularly instrumentalists who really wanted to stretch out and were being told by, let's say the 'R&B' side of the industry, that 'Black folks don't wanna hear loud guitars' and feeling the response from the rock 'n' roll side was that 'niggers can't play rock 'n' roll.'"

Established at first as a collective to help musicians gain mainstream attention, within the past twenty-five years, the group has organized several events and showcases, created a radio show, and released compilation CDs to showcase black alternative, rock, punk, and metal artists. Despite the BRC's influence, there is still a resistance to blacks playing rock music, so for women involved in the metal, hardcore, and punk scenes, the resistance is even more palpable. Though more black musicians and fans in the rock, metal, hardcore, and punk scenes have publicly acknowledged that those genres allow them to explore different sounds than those generally categorized as "authentic" black music—hip hop, R&B, soul and jazz—they must pay social and often economical price to do so.

We are now many generations removed from the blues era, but the desire to find music that matches the raw honesty of our experiences and emotions still remains. While metal does not universally contain lyrics brimming with positive reinforcement for women, or black women, the universal emotions that everyone feels are there.

IV. So You Think You're White?

I N MY LATE TEENS I WENT TO A VISIT A FRIEND who had left our hometown to attend university. I met her boyfriend, who was very popular on campus and basically a know-it-all. Steve was white, tall, and gorgeous. Despite coming from a very small town where there were few people of color, he seemed fascinated with black culture and hip hop, and he had a penchant for black women.

My friend introduced us, and as we got to know each other, he asked me about the music I liked. When I listed some alternative, punk, and metal bands, he seemed disappointed. "Where is your family from?" he asked. I explained that I was born in Toronto but adopted into a white family that lived in the same town where my friend and I grew up. "Oh. So that explains it," he said. "You're really white." "Excuse me? Do I look white to you?"

To him, I was white because my family was white, and that explained my taste in music. I responded that neither my siblings nor my parents listened to the same music as I did. Despite the lack of melanin in their skin and the number of classical musicians in my father's family, their skin color—and mine—had nothing to do with our musical tastes.

What bothered me was the presumption that I was purposefully distancing myself from my blackness, and that growing up in a predominantly white, rural environment, I had somehow lost my "black pass" along the way. That was not the first time I had been told that my musical preferences and my transracial adoptee background made me more white than black, and it wasn't even the most insulting of the several occasions. Truth be told,

I was probably better versed in black culture than his black girlfriend. I was used to having my blackness questioned. I found out who I was on my own. I knew that I had a choice: Be proud of who I was, or be swallowed by self-hate. I refused to let anyone get the better of me, and chose the former.

Despite my militant sense of self, some of the most hurtful comments I have experienced have come from boyfriends, coworkers, friends, and family members who felt more comfortable with conformity than with individuality. Black communities are bound together by sets of expectation, whether we live surrounded by black folks or not. It's hard to repeal silent codes of conduct that rule out behavior that our families and even strangers warn us about exhibiting in public.

During the 1990s grunge era, when tattoos and piercing came into fashion and even celebrities dressed in secondhand lumberjack jackets and ripped blue jeans, that prevailing fashion was not okay for everyone. I got dirty looks from black strangers for dressing in grunge chic, peppered with sneers of "dyke" and "who do you think you are?" Hell, even Marc Jacobs designed a grunge-inspired clothing line. But as a black girl who dressed the part, I was made to feel like an embarrassment to my race.

Technically, at least, not much stands in the way these days of black girls getting their hands on any music they like. All web searches are created equal, and the same goes for MP3s and digital downloads of entire albums, allowing for discovery of the widest variety of music. Teens today don't even need access to their family stereo, as was the case long ago. Thanks to portable music players and wireless laptops, parents have less control over what their children are listening to.

Yet the resistance continues on a few levels. More than ever, I'm finding black kids who never knew a time when hip hop didn't exist, and never even considered listening to anything other than what they have been told is a suitable soundtrack for black people. Hip hop is regarded either as providing a realistic narrative of urban life, or projecting the fantasy life of a singer, a producer, or a rapper.

A black metalhead can be perceived not only as an affront to the past and present struggles black people have endured, but as a personal insult to those closest to them. "Some people, especially older people, feel that you are indifferent to being black because are not listening to or respecting, quote unquote, 'our' music," says Sameerah Blue. "They think you're indifferent to your culture, you're indifferent to being a black person. They look at it as more than a series of songs, and more about the bigger picture."

Every black person in North America is somewhat aware of prevailing societal assumptions, and must struggle to rise above them. Sharing certain commonalities—like dialect, dress, dating, and music preferences—signifies to other blacks that you show pride in who you are as a black person. For anyone who chooses not to adopt those cultural signifiers for whatever reason, the choice is seen as a rejection, even an insult. The status quo has questions ready for this: *Do you think you are better than me? Why don't you want to be like us?*

In the 1903 essay "Of Our Spiritual Strivings," from *The Souls of Black Folk*, W. E. B. Du Bois wrote about the polarization between blacks and whites at that time. He identified the danger of people trying to change their identities to conform to how others perceive them, abandoning what they know to be their true selves. He described this process as "a loss that leads to self-doubt, depression, and isolation." Perceptions of black people already led to sweeping generalizations about the entire population, limiting creative and professional opportunities and hindering them from developing their individual identities. Why impose limits from within?

Though still an important issue, altering one's behavior to conform to a set of expectations and adopting a proper dialect in public are not as necessary as they were in the 1960s to ward off police harassment, workplace discrimination, or physical harm. Most likely, the parents of today's teens grew up in the post–civil rights era, with less stringent rules about how to present themselves in public in order to avoid trouble. Yet there is a sense of silent dread of someone outside black communities observing one black person acting out in a way that would negatively shape ideas about the black population as a whole.

Many of the women in this book discussing their lives in the metal, hardcore, and punk scenes felt the threat of losing their black cultural identity. They worried about being perceived as wanting to distance themselves from their culture or race. Believe it or not, blacks and nonblacks both commonly assume that black people get into heavier musical genres to shed their blackness—that we do not like ourselves and, worse, that we do not like others who look like us. Nothing could be further from the truth.

As Du Bois wrote, and Patricia Hill Collins later redefined explicitly for black women, we live with a "dual consciousness" that reconciles how we perceive the outside world with how the outside world perceives us. "The effort to interact with those who [see] you as inferior to them while remaining expressionless was and is an arduous task," writes Collins. "Behind the mask of behavioral conformity imposed on African-American women, acts of resistance, both organized and anonymous, have long existed." She specifies that black women struggle to leave stereotypes about their sexuality, physicality, and intelligence at the threshold when we come home every night.

Collins credits the arts as one of the only places where a black woman may be above criticism, whether she chooses to be a performer, a writer, or a visual artist. Instead of wallowing in self-pity, Collins suggests creating an emotional and psychological vehicle to get yourself out of the mental oppression that can hinder your life. Thinking of this creative channel in terms of heavy metal is a great way to explain Keidra Chaney's upbringing as a metal fan on the south side of Chicago. In her essay "Sister Outsider Headbanger," written for *Bitch* magazine in 2000, she says,

"I buried my metal affection at first, not wanting to seem like too much of a freak to my friends, sneaking Metallica songs in between Salt-N-Pepa and Digital Underground on mixtapes. What could I possibly find appealing about heavy metal, seeing as how it didn't reflect my life experience or cultural identity in any tangible way? And yet I think that contradiction was what appealed to me in the first place. . . . allowed me to imagine myself as . . . someone who wouldn't take shit from anyone and didn't give a fuck about rules."

When I first read Chaney's essay, I thought she could have been writing about me. Even a decade after her piece was published, Chaney still occasionally gets e-mails from young black women relieved to discover someone else out there like themselves. "The fact that we are still dealing with that in this day and age is ridiculous," she says.

Chaney admits that she didn't really know any white people until she was in university. "It was very difficult to find other people into [heavy metal]," she says. "There was the band Living Colour, and Living Colour was the only common language I could pull out for people at my school. They were like: 'Well, they can do some shit with their guitars so I guess it's all right.' But it was difficult. I still liked hip hop, R&B, and new jack swing and all that, but I had this love for metal that I had to keep hidden. I could listen to it but not get too excited from it in case someone wanted to kick my ass or call me 'that white chick' or whatever."

From a historical standpoint, black people have sometimes depended on community for survival, such as when warning others of impending danger, or banding together as powerless people during the civil rights era in mass demonstrations and boycotts to become a unified force for social and political change. Our elders sometimes had to put their own needs and desires aside in order to work as a collective. In that context, black identity can exert a powerful pressure.

"Black people have a certain type of trauma, anxiety, and fear of being consumed by white American culture," says journalist and musician Greg Tate. "There is a certain basis for it because it goes back to the slave experience. It just has a hysterical dimension to it, this late in the day, the twenty-first century. I just think it's from people not being fundamentally secure in who they are, in their ability to move freely in the society. People cling to things that they are familiar with, and things that are unfamiliar represent limits that they have imposed within their own lives."

That discomfort with the unfamiliar seems to give a black person, whether we know him or her or not, the license to tell random black strangers how to dress and behave in public. Black metalheads, especially black women, can expect to be publicly corrected regarding their behavior, through negative comments, or, in some cases, physical harassment. On some level, this dates back to the belief that the actions of one black person can negatively affect how we are perceived in the greater society.

Despite what we think about ourselves, there are those who think otherwise about us. "We always have to be in our best clothes and on our best behavior in order to win some kind of registered respect," says Yvonne Ducksworth, singer for Jingo de Lunch. "I'm a punked-out mulatto chick walking down the street. One day a car stopped and the guy seriously asked me how much I charged for an hour. I kicked his car, *hard*, rather than explain to him that I have a degree in technology and communications."

Ignoring negativity based on racial stereotypes is difficult when one is faced every day with perceived racial slights. In *Color Conscious: The Political Morality of Race*, Amy Gutmann writes that "we can neither reflectively choose our color identity nor downplay its social significance simply by willing it to be unimportant . . . but our color no more binds us to send a predetermined group message to our fellow human beings than our language binds us to convey predetermined thoughts." Amen.

Some of our parents told us that conforming was the only way to make it in North American society. "My mother's generation and my parents' generation was about making black people who were very prim and proper," says singer Camille Atkinson. "People who were very light-skinned or very dark-skinned, as they were, made sure that they never went out of the hue, made very good babies, and spread the good word of Catholicism. They didn't know that a couple of generations later, they were going to have queers, they were going to have punks, they were going to have feminists who were going to go to school for thirty years before they were going to have kids, so it shifted everyone's expectations. What it means to be black is constantly being redefined."

We watched our white schoolmates and wanted what they had. We wanted to be perceived as normal, and conventionally attractive instead of "she'd be beautiful if she wasn't . . ." We didn't want to alter our natural beauty in order to fit in. We diligently went to college or university, bought homes, straightened our hair, and made sure that we spoke right in mixed company. When we see other blacks who don't seem to be putting in the effort, we get frustrated that they could erode all the work we've done to avoid being lumped into a negative racial stereotype.

But for Tamar-kali, hardcore punk was a path to blackness. She looked at her family roots and stopped worrying about being accepted or rejected by her community. "I took the next step and started becoming aware of race in general and my history and my path in terms of being a descendant of enslaved Africans," she says. "I was interested in the history and the hardcore scene really suited the emotions that I was experiencing and the things that I was finding out. So there was definitely a lock and a seal on me really embracing the music, and leading me emotionally. The sound of hardcore matched my emotions."

Talking to people for the first time about my favorite music, I catch myself preparing for the inevitable. I mentally rehearse my replies before the questions about my musical preference arise. I find the process stressful— and I wonder if I am being paranoid for thinking I will have to defend myself. "I call it parochial blackness," says Mashadi Matabane from Emory University in Georgia, author of a blog on black women guitarists from the blues era to today. "It's something that infects our minds and our decision-making process, because it forces you to always think, 'What are they thinking about me now?' If someone asks you a question, like, 'What kind of music are you writing about?' or 'What concert you are going to?' before you even answer you are processing the expected response—'What are people are going to say?'"

By not talking about your personal tastes you can, in some cases, avoid what could potentially be a ugly situation. On the other hand, the whole thing can seem so silly and trivial. "You have practiced the response, practiced talking about it to beat them to the punch," Matabane adds. "It's this extra layer that hovers over us and has the potential to cut off what it really means to be black."

For some women, it's not even the music that causes friction among their friends and family, it's the color of the musicians. "When I was a kid I loved New Kids on the Block," says Matabane. "Everybody had something to say about it—my grandfather, my mother, the kids at school—all of them were always clear that I was not the right kind of black girl. No matter what I did, it wasn't enough. That parochial blackness is as dangerous as hell. It's dangerous, it steals your joy."

"It's really unfortunate that black people will view it as 'Well, you're trying to separate yourself from people because you don't like being black,' because it has nothing to do with it," says Erika Kristen, cofounder of FourteenG.net. "It's about what you feel, and when you're friends with people, you will have a closer connection with people who share the same likes with you, as opposed to those who don't want anything to do with it and will judge you for it. And that's the part that burns me up. I don't feel that anyone should be judging anything that you like. If you like hip hop, gospel, or even country, it's still an extension of yourself. People tend to take music very personally, which is very interesting. I know I do."

When I first met Pisso, a beautiful black woman with a proud Afro and a vast knowledge of punk and Oi! music, I was stunned that she was once involved in the skinhead scene in Chicago. She just looked very different from the stereotype I had in my head. But being involved in the skinhead scene didn't necessarily mean that you were a racist, white power Nazi. From a Caribbean family, she is fluent in German, and explains some of her experiences in Berlin, where she moved after graduating from college. "A big part of West Indian culture is to present yourself in a nice way: always clean, nice clothes. When I switched from punk to being a skinhead, my mom definitely noticed when I shaved my head. I had gone over to a friend's house and to do it, and when I got home, she freaked out. She was very upset, like I had shaved *her* hair. She was also worried for years that I might be a lesbian. I was really tomboyish, wearing boys' clothes and playing sports, so [my] cutting off my hair probably just cemented all of those fears she had.

"With my dad, it was definitely more of a problem," she adds. "He actually stopped talking to me from the time I was fifteen until I was like, twenty-something. He eventually told me that he didn't like that I was into that 'punk stuff.'"

"I started hanging out with the skinheads," she continues, "and I felt that I had a place. I always had to work, as I was going to school, and they respected that. They respected my heritage from the West Indies and they loved the music. I would hang out with them when I was eighteen, and I started college and we eventually grew apart and I started growing out my hair again. Since then, I've found myself longing to belong to a group again."

Best friends Karma Elise and Erika Kristen were lucky. They met in high school in Chicago and realized that they loved the same type of music, which eventually led to their music website, FourteenG.net. "No one understood," recalls Elise. "At least I had Erika to read magazines with, to look at pictures, and to fantasize, like 'Hey, look at this band, do you think we could talk to them about their trade?' etc. But as far as being kids, it was really rough because no one understood it. People just thought, 'Oh. You're crazy,' and of course, that you're trying to be white. I know I will always be black, and I will be nothing but my color, and I'm fine with that. I have outside interests besides going to Africa."

Writing this book, I found other black women who had felt rejected by friends, family members, or their communities because of their musical preferences.

At one point, I distributed a mass questionnaire, and nearly three-quarters of the replies described negative reactions to listening to heavy metal.

Many of the replies were predictable: "Many people say the style of music I like isn't really music, it's just loud noise. Or that I'm not black because I like rock or punk music."

Others were encouraging: "Especially when I say I like rock, they think it's like devil or white music. I find it hilarious. I revel in my musical tastes and find audio joy wherever I can."

Some were unfortunate: "When I was younger, I was criticized for listening to 'white' music and told I was weird and [that] there was something wrong with me for being a black girl listening to rock 'n' roll. . . . [Then] I learned that black folks actually *created* it."

And many stories were downright infuriating: "Especially when I was in my teens and twenties, comments from some family and friends if I was listening to rock or punk music were like: 'Why you listening to that white shit?' I once dated a white guy who grew up in a black neighborhood, and was trying to be 'down,' and he yelled at me for listening to Led Zeppelin: 'Don't you listen to any black music? Why do you listen to that white music for?'—the funniest thing I ever heard. Now that I'm in my forties, I don't tend to associate with anyone who is so narrow-minded about me or my tastes in life."

Among black women heavy metal and punk fans, there is a quiet movement to build allegiances, or at least a desire that I hope becomes reality before much longer. In the meantime, the general disapproval is strong enough to dissuade women who want to become involved from participating, and that is just sad. Rejection by friends or even family members, as Pisso mentioned, adds another layer of angst to the same trials and tribulations experienced by the white kid from the suburbs whose parents threaten to send him to private school over his Slayer and Gwar posters.

"In high school, a lot of my friends were these long-haired freaks listening to nothing but death, black metal, and rock music," says Ashley Greenwood, singer and guitarist for the New Jersey–based hard rock band Rise from Ashes. "The other black kids didn't understand who I was as a person. This one girl called me the devil because I was listening to Black Sabbath. I said, 'How can you call me the devil and say that I'm an evil person and that I'm going to hell, when you are having premarital sex with your boyfriend? Doesn't God say that you're not supposed to do that? Who's the hypocrite?' She got very upset about that."

"I get that to this very day," says Sameerah Blue. "Part and parcel of the reason that I hid albums under my mattress when I was younger wasn't necessarily because of my parents. My folks are really cool people, so while they didn't understand what I was listening to over time, they just thought, 'Whatever.' The reason I would hide my albums was because I would get shit from my black friends—'the wannabe white girl.'"

When hardcore fan Monique Craft was younger, she would tell people that she was half German and half Dominican to counter the questions about why she was listening to the music. "They would say, 'Oh, that makes sense. It's *okay* now for you to have a full-sleeve [tattoo], because it would be really weird if you were all black and listened to that type of music.' It makes you feel like an outsider but in the wrong way, like if I let them know that I am 100 percent African-American, then it would be even weirder, and then I would be even more of an outcast. It shouldn't be like that. It's just music."

The need to find a place to fit in is universal, and many black women experience painful emotions when they are made to feel ashamed of their involvements in the metal, punk, and hardcore scenes—the only places where they truly feel they belong.

"I think that disgust is there because it's human nature to look down at things that we don't understand," explains Elise. "Unfortunately, there are a lot of black people who are not exposed to other types of music within the household they grew up in. I was fortunate that I was, and got into the whole 1980s music explosion.

"I saw the trend of every one of my friends who were into R&B music who refused to even go down that road of 'Maybe there's something else that I possibly could like,' because their parents weren't into it, but just because your parents weren't into it doesn't mean that you can't like it. But because it's something that you're not used to, people tend to turn their back on it, and it's a shame, because it's something that you are really missing out on."

Black cultural theorists and black media outlets have even taken up the question of whether rock music in general is too white for black people. In the fall of 2009, I anticipated visiting the Midwest to attend a conference on the black representation within rock 'n' roll music. The event would be one of very few social gatherings on the subject, but I had a nagging feeling that the experience might not be as productive and enlightening as I wished. Even before getting on the plane, I had questions about the focus of the conference.

I was unsure of some basic operating principles. For example, would "black rock" encompass all blacks performing regular rock music? Or would the term apply to some hybrid of rock and hip hop? Would rock be treated as black-originated music or not? Would the bands discussed consist of entirely black folks? Within rock music, would black artists from the metal and punk genre be included? Or would "black rock" be an catchall including black artists creating nontraditional music and culture that had nothing to do with rock?

On the first day, my fears were legitimized—the definition of "rock" was based more on a philosophy than on actual black rock music. The idea of the music was far better than the execution. I felt out of place. I challenged Netic Apocolypto of Game Rebellion that he seemed more concerned with making a name for himself than with creating music, and the people around me looked at me like I had lost my mind. I could feel the voices saying *Who is this weird woman who loves white music?* reverberating through the hallowed halls of the university sponsoring the conference. Immediately afterward, I flew to New York to a metal show, where, despite being the only black person in the West Village club, I felt more at ease.

Black rock bands such as Living Colour, Fishbone, the Noisettes, and TV on the Radio have enjoyed popularity over the past twenty years, but in total they point to no clear-cut definition. I've seen Living Colour and Fishbone live, and though to me they certainly qualify as "black rock" bands, the crowds were 90 percent white. I would love to hear a black rock conference address why black folks weren't attending shows by black bands, or if it even mattered who was in the audience.

"Black rock" is certainly in the eye of the beholder. Black singers and musicians whose music doesn't even remotely come near to having any rock or alternative rock music elements are lauded for having a rock attitude, and are touted as artists that young black rockers should look up to. The successful 2003 documentary *Afro-Punk: The Rock 'n' Roll Nigger Experience* served as a rallying cry for young black kids into punk music, but in that case the *New York Times* came on board and cleared a prestigious path.

I have noticed a disturbing pattern when talking about black rock to black music journalists. While the black involvement in punk music seems to be acceptable, black involvement in heavy metal is not. A punk band with just one black musician may qualify as a "black rock" band—shades of the "one drop" social classification rule—but in heavy metal even the proponents of black rock overlook the black pioneers. I routinely recommend metal bands with black members to fellow black music journalists and receive no response.

I don't believe the journalists who support black rock approve of heavy metal. Some of the music promoted on black rock sites is awful. Not only do I not enjoy the music, but it is evident that the musicians put more emphasis on how they look than on playing their instruments properly. I believe they are acknowledged and marketed because they are different—but not *too* different. A lot of bands marketing themselves as black rock are extreme in comparison to traditional black-centric musical genres, but still play it safe within the limits of black authenticity.

The idea of black people in rock is edgy and sexy, which is why hip hop artists like to pose with electric guitars, even though they do not know how to play them. Black female R&B and hip hop artists will temporarily get rid of their programmed beats and hire a live rock drummer as an excuse to don an all-black skintight outfit and pretend to be nasty for a three-minute song.

According to Roctober.com, many people in the rap community were not that fond of rap groups adopting more aggressive beats. However, because of the shared DIY philosophy, both punk and early rap music made good partners. Producer Rick Rubin has publicly repeated that when music executive Russell Simmons first heard Public Enemy, he said: "Rick, this is like black punk rock. How can you waste your time on this garbage?"

In early 2009, Afronerd.com invited director Raymond Gayle, creator of the documentary *Electric Purgatory: The Fate of the Black Rocker*, to talk about the contemporary state of black rock artists. I was pleased when Gayle and the host expressed confusion as to why black rock, punk, and metal artists cannot do what they do, reaching across racial lines however they wish. "Music is music," the host exclaimed, recounting a story about being rejected by an international film festival because the board that reviewed films for the festival was perplexed by the subject matter. "Why can't people just write the lyrics and play the music that they want?"

I understand a little resistance to loud, pounding music that incorporates screaming and yelling and references to the devil and hell. But I am outraged by the classism that stereotypes metal as music for angry, racist, sexist white men, and the snobbery that questions the racial authenticity and legitimacy of the black heavy metal fan. Are black heavy metal fans supposed to be ashamed of their taste—or should the music establishment be ashamed of their own ignorance about where heavy metal came from?

"We are simply going to say, 'This is what it is. This is what I enjoy.' Lay down the law," says Tamar-kali. "Whenever somebody says no, we have got to stand on our core experiences of being women of color. We can't separate any of this. We can't compartmentalize things because people are not used to women of color and how we live our lives. We have to set the tone of how we understand ourselves. We have to create our own framework of understanding ourselves and how we function in the world. We know our reality."

V. The "Only One" Syndrome

EAVY METAL, HARDCORE, AND PUNK MUSIC SCENES breed their own kind of conformity. On the surface, these movements are all about unity, creating communities based on musical and sometimes social and political traits, not racial ones. They are all largely male-dominated. Men are used to seeing their "own" at shows, and the image of the brotherhood is crystallized.

Though I wish it were not even a factor, my presence at metal, hardcore, and punk shows is always felt. Though black female fans of these genres purchase their tickets and travel to the venue for the same reasons as everybody else, everyone I spoke with while writing this book cited a tension that must be dealt with one way or another. Everyone also mentioned how the presence of another black person at a show can either increase or lessen that tension. Though I might never speak to the man or woman across the room, when I see another black person at a show, I breathe a sigh of relief.

Each person in the metal, hardcore, and punk scene participates at a show in different ways—some mix it up in the pit all night, others hide in the back of the club. But participating in some way is crucial to keeping the music scene alive and vital. If people are still feeling ostracized after all these years, especially as more people of color come on board, how healthy can metal and punk culture be?

In twenty years of attending concerts, I have been on the receiving end of both negative and positive—albeit sometimes patronizing—attention. At a recent appearance by legendary all-black Detroit punk band Death, a white stranger nudged me and said, "You must be so proud." Along with the uninvited attention from nonblack audience members, there is also an undeniable streak of vitriol that sometimes comes from other blacks, often the only other black person, in the room. I can understand the bad vibes from nonblack attendees, but from my own people too?

Let's face it: The opportunity to create some sort of alliance with a black stranger is important, whether building a friendship with someone who has the same musical interests, or just greeting a casual acquaintance at an occasional show. Black female metal fans already face skepticism from friends, family members, and even strangers on the street. Having a sister on the scene could be a great thing—but that connection can be tough to establish when we are too used to being "the only one."

A few years ago, my best friend and I went to a concert with a phenomenal lineup featuring Testament, Heaven & Hell, Motörhead, and Judas Priest. Between bands we milled around the outdoor arena, griping about the price of beer and checking out our fellow attendees. The bands were all well-known metal legends, and their fans ran the gamut from gray-haired headbangers, leather-covered bikers, and white-collar businessmen in vintage concert T-shirts and khaki pants, to young fans checking out the pioneers of metal for the first time.

As usual, I saw only a handful of brown faces in the crowd. Then, out of the corner of my eye I saw a young, tall, beautiful, scantily clad black woman, part of an entourage of people I knew as metal journalists and insiders. They stomped through the crowd, which parted for them like the Red Sea. My friend nudged me to approach this woman and get her story, but I hesitated.

The woman was wearing an extremely short black leather miniskirt and a fitted black leather vest, and she was covered in tattoos from head to toe. Her face was heavily made up, and she wore dog chains and tons of silver jewelry, along with knee-high stiletto boots in the sweltering heat. Her weave hung down to her ass. I watched her walk down to the front of the stage, and she was soon escorted to the backstage entrance. I had this feeling that even if I had sprinted down and caught up with her, she wouldn't have wanted to talk to me.

The following year, I saw the woman again, wearing a similar outfit, this time at a Napalm Death show. She was with a good-looking white guy who looked like he might have been her boyfriend or husband. Again, I hesitated. I didn't want to approach her. It was her outfit. I was wearing my own version of metal gear: a hoodie, jeans, and black Converse. I go to metal shows to bang my head and just chill with my friends. The other black woman was dressed so provocatively that I didn't take her seriously. She was at a Napalm Death show, after all, and most likely seriously into metal. Owing to her getup, however, I felt that she was trying too hard.

In the years since these episodes, I started feeling guilty about judging another black woman because of her appearance. More than that, I have realized that I was afraid of what *her* look might mean to *my* presence in the scene. Honestly, a bit of anxiety had washed over me both times I saw her. She came across as a somebody, and I compared myself to her on multiple levels.

I seriously wondered if putting on painful heels and leather in the middle of summer would be a good move. I wondered even harder why the hell I cared about what this stranger was wearing. And I put my brain to work, thinking about the elephant in the room: interactions between black concertgoers at metal shows. For sure I notice the few black people in the crowd. I do not need to run up and give them a bear hug or a high five, but I wonder if they share the trepidation I sometimes feel when entering a show where the crowd might be sketchy, taking their musical taste public.

N

I have felt the disheartening chill of making eye contact with the only other black girl at a metal show, and receiving a death glare in return that says, "In no uncertain terms may you even try to talk to me and embarrass me." When one is simply looking for an ally, and not looking for a "Kumbaya" moment at all, it seems preposterous to be rejected for whatever reason. Yeah, it hurts.

As an avid concertgoer, Los Angeles metal journalist Sameerah Blue describes the competition she sees between black women. "You wouldn't automatically hear 'Yay, you're like me! You're black and let's be friends!'" she says. "It would become kind of like, 'Dude, I'm the black girl in the scene. What's your problem?' You are so used to being the only one, that when there is another black girl at a show you feel territorial. If you were just walking down the street and saw another black person, [you wouldn't] just walk up to them and say, 'Omigod you are my new BFF because we're both standing by the Victoria's Secret!' At the same time, you do kind of feel a weird kinship at shows."

Even black women and men interact with each other differently. "When you see another black person, you acknowledge that you know they are there," explains Ashley Greenwood, "but you don't want someone to think that you all came together. Anyone of another race, whether Asian or Hispanic, you don't automatically think that they are with a group of their own, but for some reason, people just automatically assume that with blacks at a concert, we must all be together."

"There is this sick sense of elitism going on," adds Karma Elise. "No one said that you all have to band together because of your color, but I think that a lot of the black woman feel that 'I've done it this long, I don't need you. Just because we're black we don't need to band together.' Women who have been in the scene for so long refuse to face another stigma, because there's more of us."

But it is a lonely prospect to be "the only one," which is why the avoidance on the part of other black people troubles me. I could easily blend in at a hip hop concert, support the community, and receive all kinds of affirmation, but that's not the music I like. Particularly with regards to extreme metal, if you are one of the self-selected minority of all people into the scene, then what you look like should not be a factor! Of course, it is. "To pretend that the metal scene is colorless would be backsliding," says Sameerah Blue. "You've worked very hard to do what you've done, not to have someone just bring it back to being black. Then again, it is what it is—you will never be able to be *not* that color unless you pull a Michael Jackson. Even then, everyone will always know where you come from!"

Saying people have "worked hard" to carve out space in the metal scene, means navigating and trying to feel comfortable where most likely you are going to be at most one out of a handful of people of color. For some people that work could include mustering up courage to go to shows, alone or with friends. And it's lonely work.

"I've talked to white people who seem oblivious that racism exists," says Pisso. "I told some people that I went to a soccer game in Berlin, and some guy started making monkey noises at me in the line to get into the stadium. Some people have said to me that they don't believe that happened. In terms of racism at rock shows, if I talked to a black person about my experiences, they would be like, 'What? Why are you there with those white people?' [The implication is] that I should not have been in those spaces."

Even if black men might feel uncomfortable at times at shows, at least there are more black male musicians in the metal scene than black women. "I was a member of the guitar group in high school—the only black girl there," says Ashley Greenwood. "There were a lot of black guys, but to see another black female was a rarity. I don't know if it's because society tells you that's it's weird or out of the ordinary to be a black woman listening to rock music." Furthermore, black men don't have to worry about being seen as sex objects if they arrive at a show alone. Ands it's more likely that other men will actually want to have a conversation with them, instead of just staring at them.

Nonetheless, black men also want that special connection to others like them. Former God Forbid guitarist Dallas Coyle says that black male fans always approached him after shows. His brother Doc remains in the band, which also features a black singer and drummer. "It's really not what they say," says Dallas, "but it's more just about the connection. When you start speaking to them, they feel more comfortable, because then they realize you are just like them, and they feel better about the 'Why are you listening to this?' comments they get from others."

"Because I'm playing this kind of music, it expands the notion of who is into metal and who can play metal," says guitarist Tosin Abasi from Animals as Leaders. "There is always an unspoken camaraderie. I haven't had a lot of explicit conversations where race is brought up in the metal context, but there is always this unspoken connection. Occasionally the only black kid at the show will come up and talk to me. He doesn't have to come out and say it, but I feel that there is this little extra something. I think it is really cool, and it goes in line with expanding people's ideas about who can do what and why. And if that gives some other kid the push he or she needs to motivate them to play guitar or whatever, it's really awesome."

The presence of a black woman at a show is a little more complicated, as gender issues pile onto the racial stereotypes. Women at shows might be mistaken as looking for a one-time hookup, or for a groupie who is more interested in getting backstage. Pittsburgh-based Monique Craft has been told that she is not perceived as a threat when she hangs out her male friends at metal shows. "I've had female friends even tell me to my face that I'm not attractive enough to be jealous of," she reveals, "that they don't care if I'm hanging out with their boyfriends. They are more concerned about the girl with the miniskirt and the long blonde hair. When I was younger I used to hang out and dance with the guys at hardcore shows. At those shows there are times when there are no girls out because the guys on the floor are going absolutely insane. I could handle it. Some of the girls would get mad, go on the floor, and try to 'accidentally' push me just to let me know that they're just as tough as I am. I've gotten a lot of attitude [from] women who feel the need to intimidate just for some reason or another."

Alexis Brown from Straight Line Stitch says that the reaction from other women to her singing in a metal band is mixed. Black female fans are always excited to see her, and she makes herself available to talk to them after her set. As far as nonblack women, "You find all types, you really do," she says. "There are a lot of times that you'll be at a show and there will be beautiful girls, and you think that they are going to be catty and look at you all weird, but then those are the ones that end up loving you the most. But I've run into girls who have been catty, saying 'I don't like female-fronted bands. I think they all suck.' You can't take the good without the bad."

Erin Jackson, a longtime metal fan from New Jersey, has over many years cultivated a group of black girlfriends who have gained attention because they go to metal shows as a group. "We're all aware of the racism, but we ignore it," she says. "I find that whenever I go to a show in New Jersey, the other metalheads will let you know exactly what they think of you. They will stare at you, and at times, it's like they try to get your attention, so you will see that they are glaring at you to let you know they think that you are not welcome there."

Elsewhere, more black women in the metal and hardcore scenes often means more tension at shows. "There's been an upswing of them, yes, and it's a nice thing," says journalist Karma Elise. "However, many of the black women who are there aren't necessarily trying to acknowledge you. They will turn their heads. Even after you catch their glance, they still do not necessarily want to be around you, because they want to ignore that both of you are black."

"Because they've never confronted those issues, white people in the scene just pretend that racism doesn't exist," adds Pisso. But racism exists on many sometimes invisible levels. "It takes someone that suddenly makes them feel uncomfortable, and then all these issues surface."

N

I continued to mull over how I unfairly judged the black woman I saw at the Judas Priest and Napalm Death shows based on how she was dressed. I thought about how her clothes also made her look like she was wearing a shield; she was literally armored like a tough girl nobody should ever think about approaching. Ditching my prejudiced—and admittedly ignorant—initial observations, I wondered if she simply wanted to be different from everyone else.

I shared my story with Sameerah Blue, who said: "For women to be accepted in the metal scene as a musician you have to be able to play like a motherfucker. Or you have to be a sex tart. The girls who are in these metal bands have to work so much harder to get half the respect as a guy who doesn't play half as well. For a lot of girls in the scene, there is no medium. This woman might just like the music and the people, but dresses that way because it is expected as a woman in that scene to be hypersexual—at least in appearance."

Other black women are less circumspect about other women in their music scene. "I have definitely had hate toward women in ways where I feel like I have to be in control," says singer Tamar-kali. "We keep each other in check along the same lines as the oppressor. It's like on the plantation, or wherever we are now. After a while, you don't even have to do anything, because you have already indoctrinated them. As women, we will judge each other as whores, sluts, this or that, so at a certain point, the man can go away and we'll start taking it out on each other."

"I have seen a lot of black women in Chicago who will get into the pit," says Elise, "but that type of woman almost has to prove to the rest of the crowd that she belongs there. She has to hit harder, she has to throw her horns harder, she has to recite every single lyric to show that she belongs there. I do think that that's a travesty. Because even if you are standing on the side, it doesn't mean that you don't like that band any less than the person who is throwing her entire body into it. So there could be another flip side to that argument that you don't have to sit there and prove to every other single soul who doubts you that you belong there."

Some black women take advantage of their difference to push their own individuality. "Whenever I would go to a punk show I would wear stuff that you might wear to the disco," recalls Laura Nicholls about her days in Toronto's punk scene. "I figured that it doesn't really matter because regardless of what I wear, I'm going to stand out. I'm black and there's nothing that is going to make me fit in. It was provocation because I was like 'Fuck you, I'm here' but it was also protection because I was expressing 'No, you are not coming near me.' I felt safe because I was wearing this very loud camouflage and I wasn't going to fit in. I didn't want to deal with a lot of the assholes that go to that type of concert, so I dressed up."

"Some of us welcome the token status," admits Tamar-kali. "It makes us feel more special. I met a good friend of mine in that way. We saw each other during orientation at college and I was peeping his style. I was a really crazy Fishbone fan back then, and I could tell that he was: You could just smell [a] Bonehead—a rabid Fishbone fan—[as] another Bonehead. And so we were doing a lot of posturing and sniffing each other out. In hindsight, it was interesting how we had to test each other to see if the other one was really about it. There were tons of white kids becoming our friends and kids we were befriending without putting them through the ringer, so what's that about? It's how we validate ourselves because it's like 'I'm just automatically going to think that this kid is a poser and I'm going to test this brother.'"

In 2003, the provocatively titled independent documentary *Afro-Punk: The Rock 'n' Roll Nigger Experience* was released, telling the story of young African-Americans involved in the punk and hardcore scenes. Perhaps unwittingly, the film sparked a conversation about whether the "only one" syndrome can be beneficial. The film's website eventually drew thousands of young black men and women who actively participated in the site's message board. Due to the film's limited release, many of the forum participants did not even have a chance to view the film until years later.

I sat in the darkened theater at the film's premiere at the 2003 Toronto International Film Festival and heard strangers talking about the same issues that had affected me. The film narrates the experiences of four black artists in the hardcore and punk scene and includes interviews and music clips from both notable and obscure black rock and punk musicians. I felt both sadness and sympathy for the interviewees and a bit of relief for myself. Even though I was more a metal fan than a punk fan, I responded to a community like the one I had been looking for. Most importantly, I found out that I wasn't crazy—others had experienced the same hurt, frustration, and racial confusion as me.

Afro-Punk focused on the dynamics of going to shows, meeting people, and dating, and on the complications of being a visual minority in the punk scene. One character, college student Mariko Jones, seemed to have a prolonged effect on a number of people who had seen the film—she reveled in her "onliness" in the scene, thinking that her uniqueness benefited her. Her story angered some viewers; she seemed to be a very sensitive, emotionally immature young woman who had issues with her racial identity.

Jones believed that her biracial black and Asian heritage was not relevant to her friends and associates, and that she transcended negative racial stereotypes. Despite her constant assertions that she was proud of her ethnicity, she seemed to fully believe in those same stereotypes. She boasted that she wasn't really black, because she was middle-class, not sexually promiscuous or "ghetto," and her parents were married. The punk scene for her was a community where she was valued for being Mariko, and not for things out of her control.

Other subjects in the documentary wanted to partake in and celebrate the energy and aggression of hardcore punk and the do-it-yourself philosophy in which self-determination and entrepreneurship is encouraged. Fully participating and celebrating their black identity despite being involved in a predominantly white, male-dominated environment, they were indeed unique, but not tokens. They accepted and embraced the contradictions and confusion of their lives.

Within a year, the website's popularity increased tremendously, and it served as a forum for black youth to meet other blacks in the punk, rock, and metal scenes. One of the most pressing questions from *Afro-Punk* was: *What is up with Mariko?* In reality, Mariko Jones gave voice to common issues surrounding racial identity in musical scenes that are primarily directed toward whites. Director James Spooner had, in Mariko's portrayal, opened a window into a large, yet relatively unrecognized, problem that many young black punk fans faced.

The Afro-Punk message board assumed a life of its own, raising deeper and more intense questions as the community grew: How did others feel when they went to shows? Did they talk to the one or two other black kids there, or did it seem silly to single them out because they were black? What about interracial relationships and sexuality? After all, if you want a partner that you have something in common with, wouldn't the most obvious place to meet that person be within the scene that you favor?

Yet within the Afro-Punk forum, there was discord—based on musical preference. Metal fans felt like second-class citizens compared to the punk rock majority. "I found that black people who are into metal were pushed to the side," says metal fan Erin Jackson. "The punk kids had more coverage, but I didn't even consider their music very punk; it was more like indie and garage type of bands. Still, they pushed us metal fans out of the way. To like heavy metal means like there is something wrong with you, so you can be angry at the world, and that it's obvious that you are mad at something." Even in the nucleus of a new black musical hub, there was not room for black women heavy metal fans.

N

Black women who fall prey to the "only one" syndrome can find themselves hurting more than helping their own needs, and losing opportunities to make much-needed alliances and friendships. I definitely missed my chance to make a much-needed alliance in my hometown, because I lacked the guts to befriend the black woman I saw at the Judas Priest and Napalm Death shows. Her sexualized appearance made me wonder whether she was using her physical beauty to try and compensate for being a black woman in an all-white environment. Now I realize that was none of my damn business.

I also dress a certain way, more for practical reasons then anything else. Since I won't meet the westernized standards of beauty, I might as well try to be comfortable. I don't want to be chastised for how I look, but I judged a total stranger on how she chose to present herself.

When fans choose to dress or act in a way that represents their musical preference in everyday life, that image shifts based on the person observing them. "When I walk around the streets and I see a black emo kid, which you see a hell of a lot more now than you did even ten years ago, I'm still surprised," says professor Devon Powers. "I say that only because I see that imagery as being exceptional. It's like seeing a pink unicorn! I almost think you have to reconcile the shock that most people would feel, that's a shock that happens because it's out of place. It doesn't make sense. It's a moment of reckoning. When those moments happen, you're required to think about yourself and that other person and you become very self-conscious about identity in those moments, especially when people don't live up to your expectations, or they are doing something that seems radical."

The next generation of kids will have even more access to different styles of music, and hopefully will be even more willing to check out different scenes. Despite its lack of inclusion of metal fans, the Afro-punk movement has sparked an interest among the younger black generation in punk and rock music. "I think it's generational," says Tamar-kali. "We're getting away from it right now. I know people whose kids are like, 'So what?' about Obama's election. They didn't see how special it was. But part of our thing is that black American communities are fragile. We only unify when we need to combat a struggle."

Affirming your identity as a black woman and concertgoer in the metal, hardcore, and punk scenes can help validate your presence. That identity only grows stronger in terms of numbers, not weaker. Having someone to back up that you have every right to be there would mean you will enjoy yourself even more. If you don't like being judged, then why impose that attitude on the same people who might end up being those you could potentially hang out with? I'm pretty sure I'm not the only one to have made such a regrettable mistake.

VI. Too Black, Too Metal, and All Woman

TWO MUSIC VIDEOS FROM THE 1990S remain clear in my memory for their presentation of images of black women metal, hard rock, and punk performers crashing apart racial and sexual stereotypes. The first was the Family Stand's "Ghetto Heaven," Sure, the video is stamped with its 1990 fashion and vibe, but singer Sandra St. Victor stood out as an incredible, sensual singer who proudly showed her curves. The music was funky and raw, and so was she.

Nineteen ninety-five brought the video for "Selling Jesus" from England's Skunk Anansie. Their music is much heavier than that of the Family Stand, hard rock with a distinct electronic edge. The sight of the statuesque dark-skinned, bald, and beautiful singer Skin wearing skintight leather was incredible. With her tribal makeup and aggressive, almost demented, vibe, the entire package made sense to me. Skunk Anansie played the music that contemporary black girls should be performing. Skin's performance was built on barely controlled hostility and sensuality that emanated directly from her—not her clothes or makeup. Skin's power and confidence shot through my television set and made the hair on my arms rise.

I felt a kinship to both singers; they symbolized my fantasy of how I would want to look and act if I fronted a metal band: strong, loud, and sexual. They were in control of what they looked like and how they wanted to move, never seemed manufactured to be provocative or to convey something that they were not. Black women's bodies are eternally scrutinized in the media. We are too large and, sometimes, too dark. Our hair is different in a way that is not alluring, but wooly and unattractive. Sandra St. Victor and Skin were leagues beyond all that.

Too often, black women's bodies in hip hop and R&B videos are under the control of producers, directors, and in theory the general public. Women artists are manipulated to be what record label reps think the audience wants to see—a showy spectacle, not a living, breathing artist. St. Victor and Skin seemed proud of their bodies and their individuality. They appeared edgy compared to slim, waiflike creatures like R&B superstars Whitney Houston and Mariah Carey. They were not filling a role or just reading from a script. Both "Ghetto Heaven," and "Selling Jesus" were social and political commentaries on sex, race, and class. To me, the powerful music suited the lyrics and seemed like a perfect way to transmit this meaningful information to the masses.

While there are even more women metal and hardcore musicians than there were twenty years ago, they are still often judged on physical appearance over their talent. I argue that women have a harder time gaining credit for their musical skills. Women who are conventionally attractive can grace the cover of glossy hard rock music publications and garner attention for their bands. Otherwise, women of all ethnicities often labor in obscurity.

The black women musicians I interviewed for this book, while they acknowledged the prevailing sexism in popular music culture, admit to the power of good images of black women as metal, hardcore, and punk performers. The way black women musicians handle themselves as potential role models for budding young musicians not only affects how seriously their own images and careers will be taken, but can serve as a platform to change prevailing racial and sexual stereotypes about black women in contemporary society.

N

The beauty of black womanhood has been hard to enunciate to the general public. After all, who feels the glaring need when there is no concerted effort to promote positive images of white, Asian, or Latin women? We could just read *Vogue* and *Elle* magazines and apply those fashion standards and be done with it. Young black girls into metal could just look up to Arch Enemy's blonde bombshell Angela Gossow, after all.

In the slave era, black women were perceived as chattel, whether providing domestic or manual labor on the property of their slave owners, or fulfilling various sexual directives. They bore children that became sellable property, and they were commonly raped and beaten into submission. Black women were not "proper women," so men could use them as necessary. Though slavery was abolished, a legacy of inferiority has continued. Some people resented no longer having physical or economical control over blacks, and attempted to make their lives as miserable as possible. Despite this opposition, former slaves sought and obtained educational opportunities and good jobs, even political positions, and eventually earned the same societal and economical privileges as everyone else.

One of the most widely documented stories of the public policing of black women's bodies occurred in 1810, when South African slave Saartjie Baartman—known as the Hottentot Venus—traveled to England on the advice of the brother of her slave owner to participate in an exhibition. Not exactly knowing what she would be required to do, she had gone on the promise that she would be able to keep the money that she would make. For the next five years, she toured London, appearing naked in clubs so that the audience could view her abnormally sized rear end.

Like a lot of women in her Khoisan tribe, Baartman had steatopygia, a condition that causes excess fat around the buttock area. She also had sinus pudoris, which caused an enlarged labia. Baartman had to put her foot down, refusing to spread her legs so that the audience could get a better look at the three to four inches of skin that protruded between her legs. A social anthropologist met her and, because he found her more intelligent than expected, declared her a mixture between "the highest form of animal life and the lowest form of human life."

Baartman was encouraged to travel to Paris to make money, but was unwittingly placed with an exhibition managed by an animal trainer. After that show folded, she became a prostitute and an alcoholic. In 1815, the twenty-five-year-old Baartman died of syphilis. Her skeleton, brain, and genitals were preserved and kept on display for over one hundred years in a Paris museum, until they were removed in 1974. Decades later, after much wrangling on the part of South African president Nelson Mandela and the French National Assembly, her remains were shipped to South Africa and finally laid to rest in 2002.

In 2009, Elizabeth Alexander was chosen as the poet for Barack Obama's presidential inauguration. She is author of the poem "The Venus Hottentot (1825)," which contains the lines:

"The Ball of Duchess DuBarry":
In the engraving I lurch
toward the *belles dames*, mad-eyed, and
they swoon. Men in capes and pince-nez
shield them. Tassels dance at my hips.
In this newspaper lithograph
my buttocks are shown swollen
and luminous as a planet.

Monsieur Cuvier investigates
between my legs, poking, prodding,
sure of his hypothesis.
I half expect him to pull silk
scarves from inside me, paper poppies,
then a rabbit! He complains
at my scent and does not think
I comprehend, but I speak

Alexander gives voice to the endurance and humiliation that Baartman was thought not to possess, or that was just ignored by audiences in favor of their entertainment and pleasure. The poem captures the general silencing of black women's personal narratives at that time. Baartman's experience, while extreme, symbolizes the common assumption of black female sexuality in popular culture today. Black women are still policed—sometimes within their own black communities—as to how they should express themselves.

Patricia Hill Collins writes about a culture that silences black women in order to preserve the social, cultural, and sexual status quo in "The Sexual Politics of Black Womanhood" from *Black Feminist Thought.* "This secrecy was especially important within a U.S. culture," she writes, "that routinely accused black women of being sexually immoral, promiscuous jezebels."

Beginning in 2008, the public racist attacks against first lady of the United States Michelle Obama and her two daughters have escalated from political cartoons calling her a black militant to flat-out comparisons between her and a baboon. Across the world, women of many cultural ethnicities refer to Obama as a role model, but in the trench warfare of politics she is not immune to the basest of stereotypes about black women.

In May 2011, the blog *Scientific Fundamentalist* posted the results of the questionable study "Why Are Black Women Less Physically Attractive" by Satoshi Kanazawa. Even when retitled "Why Are Black Women Rated Less Physically Attractive Than Other Women, but Black Men Are Rated Better Looking Than Other Men?" (hardly an improvement), the essay drew a torrent of complaints, and publisher *Psychology Today* pulled the post. The writer was soon suspended from his day job as a professor, and later lost his contributor position at the magazine.

Black men also perpetrate attacks on the bodies of black women. In 2010, director Tyler Perry released his remake of Ntozake Shange's 1975 stage play *For Colored Girls Who Have Considered Suicide When the Rainbow Is Enuf,* turning the strong and determined original characters into needy, cold, and emotionally unbalanced women. The *Madea* films, starring Perry as an overweight, loud, and aggressive matriarch, as well as comedian

Martin Lawrence's *Big Momma* films, portray every negative stereotype that exists about black women. And the box office tally demonstrates that a lot of people are laughing at these caricatures.

Megadeth vocalist and guitarist Dave Mustaine, a born-again Christian and right-wing commentator, pissed off a good contingent of young metal fans when he espoused his conservative views in various interviews promoting his band throughout 2012. I took offense at his offhand bashing of black women in an *LA Weekly* interview: "I watch some of these shows from over in Africa, and you've got starving women with six kids. Well, how about, you know, put a plug in it? It's like, you shouldn't be having children if you can't feed them."

And as porn becomes more mainstream and more extreme, interracial sex films are more common and more violent. Online porn sites have arrived that specifically exploit the sexual objectification and humiliation of black women, catering to viewers who want to sexually and verbally humiliate and torture "ghetto gaggers," young and poor black women. The women are filmed eating dog food and semen-soaked watermelons, and having their faces shoved into a toilet. The videos conclude with the women crying. I doubt these "performers" knew what they were getting into when they signed the release form in exchange for payment of approximately two thousand dollars.

Do they really hate us that much?

When these messages are not challenged and action is not taken, it sends a signal that there either must be an ounce of truth to them, as black women command such little respect and have such little control or credibility that the complaints are ignored. I can only fear that that the majority of people reading or viewing these films agree with that sentiment, or that they have simply not given any thought as to how people will react, as the cultural viability of black women averages pretty low.

Despite the depressing amount of offensive representation black women in the public eye receive, black female musicians represent another way we may be seen in popular culture. As mentioned earlier, Betty Davis and then Chaka Khan provided self-assured, sexual images that were risqué and revolutionary for their eras. Joyce Kennedy from Mother's Finest was the front woman of one the earliest hard rock groups to feature black members. Labelle, the '70s super group that consisted of Patti LaBelle, Nona Hendryx, and Sarah Dash, were known for their glam rock style and their willingness to combine rock 'n' roll with societal issues that many singers in that era avoided. Did their images and music preferences stay in line with what black folks thought was appropriate behavior? No. Did they care? Probably not. In fact, their risk-taking seems to have played a substantial factor in their critical, if not commercial, success.

Many young black women heavy rock, metal, hardcore, and punk fans I interviewed for this book rate Brooklyn singer Tamar-kali, who appeared in the 2003 documentary *Afro-Punk*, as one of the most visible contemporary black female musicians. They credit not only her music, but also her image as validating their interest in rock, punk, and hardcore music. *Fader* magazine wrote: "She has created an image of oozing black female sexuality crossed with a thundering hardcore authority that has attracted a mishmash of fans: moshing white boys, moshing black boys, and, more recently, fawning, affirmation-hungry black girls."

Tamar-kali's father is a musician and got her interested in bands like Led Zeppelin and Kiss. She says that her ever-changing array of tattoos and piercings weren't adopted from the punks in her Brooklyn neighborhood, but grew from what came innately to her. "I was drawn to it but that is just because of the type of person that I am," she says. "I remember all the imagery I was exposed to as a kid through my father's *National Geographic* books and I realized the link. I connected to it in that way."

"Years ago, when I first saw her perform, it was like the world opened up," says Mashadi Matabane, a doctoral student in Atlanta who researched black women guitarists for her dissertation. "She was this brown-skinned sister with a body. She had a real woman's stomach and she had hips and thighs. And her hair! From what I recall she was bald, but she had just this little patch of hair at the top. And she was playing the guitar and singing. My mind was blown. Seeing her was so powerful because she just blew open my understanding of the cultural rhythms surrounding black womanhood. She represents a link between black rockers and black pride."

Not all black women take to the stage so naturally, and the challenges are many. Perceptions of women in the metal, hardcore, and punk scenes can help the ascent—or deter women from participating at all.

A few years ago, I found a discussion board thread titled "Beautiful Black Women" on a well-traveled heavy metal website. The first post contained pictures of well-known black female celebrities, like movie star-turned-metal-singer Jada Pinkett Smith from Wicked Wisdom, along with other black women, many light-skinned, with long, straightened hair.

A number of people added their comments. Some added additional pictures that they'd found on the Internet of black women they found attractive. Most were models, not musicians, and all were light-skinned. Before I had scrolled to the very bottom, I found the comment that I feared: "Black women are not beautiful." Another comment posted after that repeated the statement and added: "Sexy, but not beautiful." I wondered what someone who could post this mildly offensive statement on a message board for metal fans must think of black female metal musicians. Though sexual attractiveness is not a musical prerequisite, judging by pictorials in music magazines, "good looks" do still matter.

Some women metal fans will profess their lust for musicians like Joe Duplantier from Gojira or Troy Sanders from Mastodon. As far as the largely male metal fan base is concerned, however, musicians need not even bathe or wear fashionable clothing to gain respect. These guys only need to "bring it," and be proficient enough at their instruments to gain credibility. For women, it's a whole different beast.

As in every other music culture, whether we like it or not, imagery is important. We can't help but react to a musical style based on the physical appearance of the performer. Because of the turbulent history regarding black women in westernized culture, "sexy, but not beautiful" is more than someone's personal sentiment. Black women are more likely to be viewed as sexualized creatures to be used and discarded.

The damage from sexual objectification within North American history, coupled with the lack of variances in the narratives of black female life outside of racially prescribed categories and the hypersexualized images of black women in hip hop culture have created a legitimate level of hypersensitivity among many black women. Without mentioning a specific genre, I individually asked a large group of black women if music affected their self-confidence or sexuality at all. I received some eloquent responses like this one: "If you look at hip hop nowadays it is all about creating a black Barbie doll illusion in little girl's heads. It seems the more hip hop progressed, the more black women lost themselves and the independence they fought so hard for. With metal I have had the opportunity to come across women who are comfortable in their own skin. There is no such thing as being a freak, just being an individual."

I was surprised when the prominent metal label Century Media Records published the Girls of Century Media 2009 calendar featuring female metal musicians on the label. All the pictures featured young, attractive white women, some dressed in those god-awful plaid miniskirts with numerous pleats, traditionally created for young Catholic schoolgirls but here hiked up so high you could see their panties—or, in this case, thongs. Others wore tight-fitting tops knotted under their breasts, outfits were that standard "rocker chick" garb available at any low-rate clothing store franchise.

The pictures seemed lightweight; I've seen more scandalous outfits on women walking down the street in the summertime. Yet to me the calendar signified a setback for women, considering it arrived during an era with probably the most skilled female musicians since metal first emerged on

North American shores. Women are represented throughout the myriad of subgenres under the metal umbrella, from the most visceral to the most technical.

Singer Militia Vox has modeled for a number of cosmetic and beauty companies, such as Manic Panic, Paul Mitchell, Shiseido, and Urban Decay. "People ask me why I don't dress that provocatively, and it's because I don't have to. People look at me anyway. *Maxim* asked me to do a pictorial for them, and I didn't because I didn't have to. In the '80s, Lita Ford was one of the best female guitarists around. And she didn't need to be sexual, but her label pressured her to be this sexual goddess. I distinctly remember seeing this video where she was licking this huge ice block. She must have known that she didn't have to do that."

The bright side of the Century Media calendar and *Revolver* magazine's "Hottest Chicks" franchise is that at least finally there are enough women in the metal scene to even fill twelve months. Lacuna Coil's singer Cristina Scabbia has appeared in a number of *Revolver* issues. She is also a contributing editor and has written a dating column for the magazine since 2005. A beautiful Italian singer who exudes a strong-willed persona, she graced the cover of the 2007 "Hottest Chicks in Metal" issue. Afterward, Lacuna Coil joined the Hottest Chicks in Metal package tour.

During the tour, Scabbia explained how she viewed her role as a "hottest chick in metal": "It was a good idea promotion-wise to use the same name [of *Revolver's* annual issue]. I like to look at it in an ironic way, especially with a lot of preconceptions that some people have about females in a band. I look at it like, 'We're chicks, but we can kick your ass,' basically."

I wonder what responsibility Scabbia felt as a role model for young women while perpetrating female stereotypes in a predominantly all-male musical genre. She was a pioneer for a specific generation of women metal fans and musicians, and I would expect her to portray herself in a manner that serves as a positive example for young aspiring female musicians. I understand that is not fair if it limits her individual freedom. On the other hand, until the percentage of women equals the percentage of men in the metal scene, the smattering of successful women musicians, regardless of ethnicity, represent the rest of us.

After all, the pioneering black women in hard rock like Nona Hendryx and Joyce Kennedy of Mother's Finest stood up for their beliefs in the 1970s, and still do today. "They practiced what they preached," says singer and professor Kudisan Kai. "They are strong, forthright women who are very clear about who they are, and true to that, regardless of what is going on around them. It's hard to find that kind of integrity within the music industry."

Journalist and metal publicist Kim Kelly wrote about "Hottest Chicks"–type press coverage in "The Never-Ending Debate over Women in Metal and Hard Rock" for *The Atlantic*. "Ostensibly, the goal is to provide exposure to the women of metal, and celebrate them for their talent and brains as well as their beauty—think Miss America's 'scholarship' competitions with less world peace and more devil horns," she wrote. "But the ladies' musical backgrounds and achievements often play second fiddle to their luminous cheekbones or dangerous curves."

Kelly took exception to Revolver's 2011 "Hottest Chicks" issue with Evanescence singer Amy Lee on the cover—not a metal artist by a long shot. Any number of talented women involved in actual metal, despite the salaciousness of the issue, went unnoticed. And the concept seemed to have legs. "The sheer volume of 'women in metal' articles proves that despite the undeniable importance of their contributions and ever-increasing presence within the scene, female metallers are still seen as something of a novelty, often a gimmick used to market the genre to the mainstream."

Very likely weary of the annual complaints, *Revolver* editor Brandon Geist issued a Twitter message to try and defend the decision to continue publishing the monthly pictorials and annual special issue. "The real point here is 'Chill the fuck out.' I'm flattered that some people think that *Revolver* has such a huge influence on society and the 'scene,' but really all we're trying to do is put out a fun issue that spotlights some rad female musicians without taking ourselves too seriously and getting all didactic 'Women in Rock' on anyone. But again, if you wanna get your panties all in a bunch about it, that's fun to watch, too." While Geist showed he isn't taking himself or his magazine too seriously, he's not taking women metal musicians seriously, either.

Since 2009, only one black woman has been featured in Revolver's monthly "Hottest Chicks" pictorial. Straight Line Stitch's Alexis Brown appeared in the April/May 2011 issue, and she submitted the photos herself, and chose her own clothes, jeans, and T-shirts. "I don't know how other girls deal with it, in terms of sexuality," she says, "but now there seems to be more sexuality. They say 'sex sells,' and then you've got Revolver's Hottest Chicks in Hard Rock. It is what it is. It's not something that I really buy into; it's great when people think you're 'hot,' but whatever. What you see is what you get. I'm not trying to look sexy. I'm not going to come out in hot pants. It's about being comfortable and putting on a show."

Says Tetrarch guitarist Diamond Rowe: "The women are good-looking and know how to rock, but it does put them in the place of being good-looking chicks trying to do what the guys are doing. They don't have the hottest guy in metal, so it should be an equal thing. It puts women in a place that keeps them separate, that they will never be as good as some of their fellow male musicians. Angela Gossow from Arch Enemy was in that, and she has one of the best vocals in her field, but referring to her as a 'hottest chick in metal' makes her inferior to her peers."

While a black woman fronting a metal, hardcore, or punk band would have to be pretty phenomenal to change the entire cultural fabric of western society, St. Victor from The Family Stand, Skin from Skunk Anansie, Brown from Straight Line Stitch, and Rowe from Tetrarch stood on principle and will hopefully bring more young black women into metal, challenging the myths that deter many black fans from following their instinctual interest toward unbridled heavy metal bliss.

In her 1991 book *Heavy Metal: The Music and Its Culture*, sociologist Deena Weinstein posited that seeing female metal artists onstage is actually a jarring experience for many male fans, as it alters the traditional norm where men play prominent, powerful roles. She believes a woman leading a band can be disconcerting for metal fans. It's safe to say that applying Weinstein's scenario to black women in metal, hardcore, and punk, the same men might have an even harder time comprehending a black women in a dominant role onstage.

Bassist Urith Myree of Dormitory Effect has opened for Black Sabbath and Jamey Jasta of Hatebreed's solo project, and has played at major music festivals and showcases. Despite being a black woman in a nearly all-male scene for twenty years, she remembers hearing very few negative comments about her presence. But one major incident has stayed with her. "Right before Dormitory Effect formed," she says, "I was in a band that included a male singer. The singer was a bit difficult, but whatever—he had 'lead singers' disease. He was a bit of an asshole. We got to the point where we had a CD being produced, and we had this big band meeting.

"The meeting turned out to be a conversation that boiled down to: 'We cannot have Urith in the band anymore.' I was like, 'Excuse me?' He said, 'Image is everything right now, and when you look at pictures of bands, they all look a certain way. It's nothing personal. I don't think it's going to work out because people are not going to want to *see that*.' 'What are you talking about?' I said. 'Well, nowadays every band is a band of white guys.' He pointed toward another band member. 'She's got the tattoos and the dreads, and she's got something cool about her, but I don't think it's going to work out with you. I think we need to get somebody else.' Everyone was like, 'You can't be serious.' But he was serious, because I was not some proverbial white kid. I said, 'You're kidding me. You're kicking me out of a band that I helped found and I was the one that suggested that you sing in it?' 'Oh well, I think that it's just in the best interest of the band,' he said. I thought that they might kick me out. But the other members said, 'Either she's in the band or we're all out, and you're an asshole.' And that was the end of that. We had all these CDs that we couldn't put out because the band broke up four weeks later. At the time, I was hurt. I cried and I was insulted, but everything worked out. If it wasn't for that incident I wouldn't be where I am now."

NYU professor and author Maureen Mahon also believes that a black female holding a key position in a rock or metal band is commonly perceived as an invasion of a man's space. "Generally, when women play instruments in mixed-gender bands, they play bass or keyboards," she writes in *Right to Rock*, "honoring a universally understood prohibition against women playing the guitar."

Diamond Rowe started playing guitar with Tetrarch as a teenager. "I don't rely on the fact that I'm a black girl playing metal. I want people to just think that I'm a great player, not a good black female guitar player," she says. "That's why I'm always trying to perfect my craft. But people do assume that I play bass or I just sing. They are always surprised that I play guitar and write."

Primarily known as a Hollywood actress, married to an A-list movie star since 1997, Jada Pinkett Smith shocked a lot of people when she temporarily set aside her Malibu lifestyle to sing for Wicked Wisdom, a nü-metal band that opened for Britney Spears in 2004 and then joined the 2005 Ozzfest tour. As *MTV News* reported, the tone on the Ozzfest message boards did not bode well for a red-carpet reception: "Wicked Wisdom will be pelted by every loose object on the Ozzfest grounds. This is going to cause a f---ing riot. . . . [B]ring your steel-toed boots."

Billboard reported that the band sensed the decision to join Ozzfest was proving more contentious than expected. Pinkett Smith defended her choice to perform. "I just love the freedom of metal music," she said. "It's not confined, really. You can express your joy, your pain, your anger and everything, so the passion of it is what attracts me the most."

Wicked Wisdom was certainly capable, but the band's melodic, almost goth-sounding style was a little too soft for Ozzfest. Most felt that because Pinkett-Smith was already known as an actor, she didn't have the metal "cred" generally earned by years of slogging it out on the road. For example, the band appeared on the *Late Show with David Letterman*, an unheard-of honor for any metal band barely two years into their career. "It went too far, too fast," says BRC president LaRonda Davis. "There was no way that a band that had just started should be on Ozzfest. There was no proving ground. The production on the record was shit. I understand you are already huge as an actress, but unless you are *the shit* already, it's not going to be easy. As a musician, do some smaller things first. It was the wielding of influence without the warranting of position."

Yet plenty of untested bands win morning-hour opening slots on touring festivals; not as many feature only black members. Furthermore, Pinkett Smith dressed down in sweats and bandannas. She almost seemed tough. "If you are going to be at Ozzfest, you would just have to be a hot chick," says Davis. "The fans just want to see the bands that they love, or at least a hot chick who's acting like she's doing some heavy shit. If they thought Jada was hot, then fine, but what I think was more important was that she could rock out."

"I think that Jada changed some minds," says metal fan Erin Jackson, a regular Ozzfest attendee. "If there hadn't been such negative feedback about the music, and if she had stuck with it, she would have had more people supporting her. The majority of the negative reaction to her had to do with race, because if she had been any other actress it wouldn't have been a big thing. I checked the Ozzfest boards that year and I had never seen so many people using the n-word before, talking about killing her, using the old 'watermelon and collard greens' racist insults. They even had to take Wicked Wisdom's message board down. As far as authenticity, I think people were also upset because she was Will Smith's wife, she used her money to get a tour bus, and everything they got came from her pocket. Will Smith was there, and he is so corny. People got mad over a picture of him throwing up the horns."

"I think people just needed a minute to get their reality on what the hell was going on," Pinkett Smith told the *San Diego Union-Tribune*. "It's a difficult thing to reconcile. This chick that you've seen play Carla Purty in *The Nutty Professor* is now in this so-called metal or heavy rock band."

"This is the problem," says Tamar-kali of her time fronting a hardcore band. "We can't fill that space because it is going to turn it on its head. I know that was behind some of the rejection I got from the male fans of the genre of music I did. If I were a boy, they'd be down with that shit. I think that it's okay to admire and to want to be like a man if you want to play, but to see a woman up there it's not even about jealousy. The people in the audience feel inadequate because this chick is rocking hard and they can't even play!"

For music journalists and A&R people who are thinking about how to categorize bands, placing a black woman into the metal, punk, or hardcore categories is confusing. Before Skunk Anansie announced their reunion in 2009, Deborah Dyer, aka Skin, had an active solo career, putting out two albums in the prior five years. This well-known hard rock singer with penchant for warrior-style makeup gained an impressive amount of attention for her fearlessness. As the principal songwriter for Skunk Anansie, she wrote lyrics about romantic relationships, racism, and politics, not shying from controversy; her delivery ranged from sweet coos to primitive screams. While the style of music the band performed could be classified as metal, punk, or even indie rock, journalists just seemed confused, classifying the band as "funk metal," "rock/soul," or the ill-fated blend of hip hop and metal known as "nü-metal"

Skin was frustrated with being a square peg in a world of round holes, as she told an interviewer in 2011: "The Americans tried to pigeonhole us. We were an R&B band in America, I kid you not! Once, on a flight over there, one of the American record execs from one of the labels we were going to see was on the plane. He asked us if we were in a band and told us: 'When we get back I'm going to introduce you to the head of the black music department.' We were like, 'Why?' We're a rock band.' It went straight over his head. Sure enough, we went to the label and got introduced to the wrong guy."

Skunk Anansie had no overt black cultural music references, but the music business could not cope with that reality. "It was just hard back then for Americans to look at me, and understand that I'm not an R&B singer, and I can't rap," says Skin. "It was very segregated. There were no white rappers or black rockers. Of course there actually were, but they weren't taking us seriously. There was a whole scene of black rock music going on at that time, bands like Living Colour. They had to try and club together and knock on the door of the big radio stations. It was very difficult for us all out there."

The rock 'n' roll theme song for the sexual availability of black women has to be the Rolling Stones hit "Brown Sugar," from the 1971 album *Sticky Fingers*. Though model and writer Marsha Hunt, who had a daughter with Mick Jagger, claims the song is about her, for the broader public the song celebrates the beauty and sexual desirability of black women—with a racist, misogynist overtones suggesting that black women are meant to be used and then discarded. In heavy metal, everything is amplified. Imagery and representation become even more important. The decisions by a black woman onstage not only convey immediate messages to the audience, but leave impressions that can easily perpetrate stereotypes that could make it harder for other black women entering the music scene.

In contrast, I have spoken with a number of black women about how hip hop culture and contemporary culture today view black women. In the mid-1990s, women were referred to in lyrics and commonly portrayed in music videos as gold-digging whores and hood rats out to fleece rappers of their hard-earned money. The general assumption was that these half-naked women were allowing themselves to be objectified. Nobody mentioned the pressure these women felt to catch an all-important break in order to segue into other opportunities in the entertainment industry.

In the mid-1990s, Public Enemy's Chuck D lectured at the University of Toronto about the state of hip hop, which at that time was at its peak. He spoke about race relations and politics, and provided some personal musings on the current batch of hip hop artists. I prepared some specific questions beforehand, and positioned myself in the front row on the balcony over the stage. When he was ready to take questions from the audience, I stood up and waved until he acknowledged me.

I asked his opinion on the present portrayals of black women in hip hop culture. For a second, he just stared at me, and then he asked me to clarify, as though he didn't know what I was talking about. I mentioned one hip hop artist who had a song in heavy rotation and had made some sexist remarks in his album and during interviews.

To my surprise, Chuck snickered and rolled his eyes. "Look, I have a wife and daughters, and I don't think that just because one artist says something it means he is talking about my kids. If women don't like that he is using his freedom of speech to talk about his experiences, that they shouldn't listen to the music." There was a smattering of applause from the predominantly male audience. Strangely enough, he seemed particularly annoyed at my question, and he continued speaking, explaining that there were plenty of lowlife women in the hood whose actions were in line with what that particular artist talked about in his album.

I was stunned. First, as rap and hip hop ruled the charts, it stung that "black America's CNN," as Chuck D once described rap, would paint any black person under the age of forty so negatively. When well-known rappers talked about women, it was felt by women, regardless of their class, status, or locale. We knew these dudes were talking about *us*—especially the younger generation, who found their black boyfriends emulating the attitudes of the rappers they admired.

Chuck D's lame response angered me. He seemed to agree with some sweeping generalizations about black women. In hindsight, I shouldn't have been all that surprised, but all I could think was how I first recognized the powerful combination between race and music through Public Enemy and their forerunners Run-DMC. I remembered how Chuck D's lyrics resonated with me, expressing the frustration and powerlessness I felt while facing racial tension in high school. His messages that black people have to unify and work together for the betterment of the race had motivated me to start reading about some of the writers and black thinkers that he rapped about. So, really, *what the fuck*?

Was the unity he encouraged directed exclusively toward men? Didn't he think better than to publicly degrade black women? As a now former devotee to Public Enemy, why the hell would I support an artist if they did not respect me as a woman? From the balcony that night, I pressed him to elaborate, but he dismissed me, turning his back to address the crowd. "Next question!"

Young listeners of N.W.A, Ice-T, and Onyx might have found the hypermachismo and harder, more aggressive beats attractive, but the private lives of the performers left a lot to be desired. In the early days, black female rappers like Monie Love, Roxanne Shanté, Queen Latifah, and Canada's Michie Mee provided positive images of talented women working in the music industry. These female rappers were just as good as, if not better than, their male counterparts. But something changed in the mid-1990s with the arrival of a new crop of female rappers like Lil' Kim and Foxy Brown. Wearing very little, they boasted about sexual exploits instead of their intellects. While they could arguably represent a kind powerful woman that could be just as raw and nasty as their male counterparts, their physical appearances as a rule overshadowed their talents.

When video vixens became popular, and hip hop lyrics changed from schoolyard taunts and odes to girlfriend problems into profanity-laced misogynist tirades, persistent complaints from female rap fans and the few female music journalists working in mainstream urban publications took back the musical landscape. Today, however, rap artists like Los Angeles–based Odd Future employ over-the-top lyrics about raping and beating women. Perhaps out of desperation, the rap scene has become like Florida death metal band Cannibal Corpse—shocking and purposefully provocative.

In 2007, Jeff Johnson wrote an opinion piece about sexism in hip hop for CNN.com. "Lyrics that were at one time provocative and merely suggestive are now blatant and overtly obscene. These images attempt to pass off the objectification of black women specifically as 'true beauty' in the name of entertainment. These images and lyrics, while acceptable for adults, are targeted to a demographic made up of young people ages twelve to sixteen. Studies have shown that these images and, more importantly, these lyrics, play a role in how young people view themselves and process sex and relationships."

In the metal, hardcore, and punk scene, black women, like singer Felony Melony from the Las Vegas punk band the Objex can come across as just as risqué as any video vixens, but they are perceived in a different light. For sure, they have a great deal of inner strength and determination to actively participate in a culture where there are very few black people. Just like Lil' Kim and Foxy Brown in the early days, they embody a feeling of empowerment as they stand in front of a crowded room of men, being themselves, shedding all the social stereotypes swirling around in the outside world.

Furthermore, metal, hardcore, and punk lyrics generally cover broader territory than boasts about sexual prowess, allowing a broader range of images and identity. Says journalist Sameerah Blue: "It's possible for black women in metal to explore a more positive side of sexuality as sensual beings, that you may not get in the realms of hip hop or R&B, where the music is hypersexualized. You can bring a completely different type of sexuality to the music that the music doesn't necessarily have."

Making that leap is still complicated, and fraught with emotional challenges. The extreme musical genres are known for corralling social outsiders into a group whose common bond is music. I would think that these people would, in theory, be protective of their fellow audience members, but it doesn't always work out that way. Black women have legitimate reasons for not wanting to attend shows, and being harassed because some idiot perceives them as being more sexually available plays a huge factor.

Some black female musicians have encountered male audience members who react to them as though they are simply an extreme version of what they have seen in hip hop videos. "There are black people who are more familiar, seem more homegrown to white people, like R&B or hip hop artists," explains Tamar-kali. "But we in the rock world are different so we sometimes draw the deviant vibe—fringe, S&M-type folk that automatically gravitate toward you because they think you fall into the dominatrix type. That's a sexual stereotype for the black women in rock, but that's a very fringe group of people."

Myree gets unwarranted comments on her physical appearance simply for being onstage. "It was tough when I was growing up and I was always told, 'Don't put yourself out there, cover yourself, try not to be sexy, try to present yourself a certain way because they will look at you like you're some type of animal,'" she says. "When I'm onstage, I don't dress sexy. People tell me that I am very sexy but if it's because I am expressing something in the music, I don't know. I have a tendency to wear football jerseys and big sneakers, but there are people who just think that women onstage who are really good musicians are just sexy."

Laura Nicholls resented the hypocrisy she saw at shows in the Toronto punk scene of the 1980s. "One of the things that makes me angry is that as a black woman I'm not allowed to own my sexuality," she says. "Taking drugs is not exclusive to black women. Being promiscuous is not exclusive to black women. White women can be irresponsible, and that is totally acceptable."

On the other hand, writing for the *Chicago Sun-Times* during the 1970s, Cynthia Dagnal-Myron was often the only black journalist, male or female, on tour and backstage at legendary rock and metal shows. She wore her hair in an impressive Afro and had access to superstars of the day like Kiss, Roger Daltrey of the Who, and Steven Tyler of Aerosmith. Dagnal-Myron admits that her success could have come down to her attractiveness, but she also credits her blackness as a plus in the early hard rock scene. "Initially, I was treated better than everyone else and to this day, I don't know why," she says. "They were delighted—I was a cute little kid, a good-looking little girl. They were curious. Maybe I represented where rock 'n' roll came from, and most of the British bands knew that. They were glad to have someone represent."

Many of the musicians I've talked with believe the benefits of playing the metal they love outweigh the negatives. "There is social stigma with black women that goes back to how we were raised to survive in this world," says singer Saidah Baba Talibah. "We are told, 'Don't be too sexual, because we don't want people to think that we're ultrasexual.' Or we are not to be sexual at all. But there is a certain empowerment behind being able to put on what you want and just wear it, but not be dictated [to] by the men around you. On one hand, it is our responsibility to monitor other black's women's appearances, but on the other hand, it's not. We have to be happy for ourselves. To live and to just *be*."

The contemporary crop of black women metal, hardcore, and punk musicians express their personalities and claim their bodies as their own. As portrayed sporting a Mohawk, facial piercings, and tattoos in the *Afro-Punk* documentary, Tamar-kali oozes confidence and an unrestrained sensuality. Her presence is organic and formidable. Lisa Kekaula from the L.A.-based hard rock band the Bellrays sports a full Afro reminiscent of forerunner Betty Davis, and she unabashedly flaunts her sexuality in front of predominantly all-white crowds. Alexis Brown of Straight Line Stitch switches between death metal growls and clean singing onstage while violently spinning her hair in a spiral. Equally unconcerned with gaining acceptance, Tetrarch's Diamond Rowe matches impressive musical talent with shrewd business sense and determination.

Rather than wait for the musical climate to change, black women are taking matters into their own hands. In 2008, LaRonda Davis produced the Primordial Punk 2009 calendar, featuring Tamar-kali, Vox, and ten other black female alternative musicians and artists. Each photo shoot was inspired by a song by a black rock band about a black woman—for example, "Sheba" by the Bad Brains. The BRC also put on events to highlight black women musicians and performers. "Our whole thing is that there are a lot of black girls who have piercings, tattoos, and Mohawks, and they are beautiful, too," Davis explains. "They're not Suicide Girl model material, simply because they're black. We wanted to appreciate them. Our friends have ink, and they're beautiful and talented, so why not reclaim those things and create something that celebrates us? We decided to take an aesthetic that people know and usually associate with the demure white girl and show these really fierce, beautiful women in a different way."

Most likely, we will never see another situation where a black woman's genitalia are reluctantly put on display for public ridicule like Saartjie Baartman's were. But public policing of black women's bodies, intellect, and behavior continues. Unlike in Baartman's era, we now have more control over how we choose to display our bodies. More importantly, we have the ability to challenge the societal limitations regarding how others perceive us. However, I believe there will always be women who choose to actively embody racial and sexual stereotypes for their own material gain. Those individuals will reap the benefits, while making it harder for other women to be seen as legitimate musicians.

As of now, there are still few black women musicians in metal, hardcore, and punk bands, but the ones that exist have the power to shatter the sexual stereotypes that have hindered black female participation in metal, simply by being themselves and by providing an alternative to what the current norm. While there will always be challenges and setbacks, the more positive images that are available, the more the younger generation of black women will participate. The problem is, where are they now, and how can we get more of them started?

VII. The Lingering Stench of Racism in Metal

IN THE FALL OF 2011 I WENT TO SEE Kyuss Lives! play in Toronto. I was planning to review the show, and I had my camera. Following the three-song limit in the photo pit, I hung out inside the barrier in the front of the stage and watched the rest of a great show. Still riding a musical high from that performance, I decided to leave immediately to beat the after-show rush. As I made my way through the crowd to the exit, suddenly a big white guy jumped in front of me and screamed, "You fucking nigger!" in my face.

My great mood vaporized. I was so stunned that I couldn't even speak. My legs felt like cement, but I kept walking. I realized that all the people who I was passing were looking at me. I felt humiliated. As I rode the subway home, I grew more ashamed at all the people looking at me; somehow that hurt more than the asshole getting in my face. I wished at that moment that there had been some other black folks there. Why, I don't know. Would they have suddenly appeared so we could all beat the guy up together? Would more of a black presence have stopped him from saying what he said? All I knew was that I desperately wanted someone with whom to commiserate.

That incident was not my first brush with overtly racist people in the metal scene, but it caught me off guard. More than once, I have wondered, "Why the hell am I putting myself through this bullshit?"

Other black women have overcome the friction at metal shows by projecting a strong image. They have told me that the more their presence is felt in the clubs and other venues, the more people will think it is normal to see them there. While I think I have a solid sense of who I am and what I stand for, these incidents test me to the limit. I want to go to fewer shows, not more. I start to feel tired of putting myself in situations that can be fraught with tension, and surrounding myself with people might never accept me because of the color of my skin and my gender.

When I tell friends who are not into heavy music about some of my experiences at live shows, they assume the situation would be scary and ask, "Why did you go in the first place?" An uncomfortable number of black folks feel that most, if not all, metal musicians and fans are rabidly racist. Ironically, they engage in a form of profiling. People who look like metalheads or punks are the people my black friends would cross the street at night to avoid. To be quite honest, there are musicians and fans out there that prove them right.

Hardly anyone will admit that the color of the musicians plays a factor in what music they choose to listen to, or that the makeup of a concert crowd can deter black people from checking out bands. Discussing racism in music is not easy, even in this supposedly postracial society after Barack Obama. Regardless of our cultural and ethnic makeup, we can download whatever music we feel like buying and become hardcore fans in the privacy of our homes. If we want to avoid potential incidents at shows, we can stay clear, but the live experience is central to the enjoyment of heavy music. Race and racism shouldn't block our ability to socialize with other music fans. Enjoying music is a universal right and a pleasurable one, but there are times when the problems of the outside world seep in and ruin the experience.

Communities of metal fans are needed in order for the culture to survive and thrive, especially in an era with such an overbearing Top 40 pop music culture. Fans of more underground and extreme music know that our favorite bands will not often profit from large sponsorships or appear at Madison Square Garden. Rock stars don't live the way I thought they did in the '80s, with a fleet of luxury cars, a few mansions scattered around the world, and mounds of caviar and cocaine waiting for them backstage after every sold-out stadium show. In order to support the bands, distribution of their music, their ability to tour, and the media outlets that keep the system moving forward, fans are essential—and these bands need all the fans they can get.

Deterring any fan from participating in metal, hardcore, and punk is simply not economically viable. But the welcome mat is not always out for black women fans. We continue to persevere, though the glares, the stares, and, unfortunately, the verbal and physical altercations that come with being somewhere where, for whatever reason, somebody feels we don't belong.

When Barack Obama became the first African-American president of the U.S. in January 2009, many people thought that a new age would begin: Institutional, systemic, overt, and covert racism would miraculously disappear and the Western world would finally offer equality for all of its citizens. People didn't take into account an ongoing economic recession, and that the stress of people losing their jobs and homes would bring more racial strife. Attending concerts in the States, I noticed a heightened tension at shows on the part of white fans, and wondered if others had felt the same. For the first time, I thought there might be truth in the stereotype of the blue-collar, angry white dude in metal.

"I think a lot of people thought it would bring America together," says Dallas Coyle, former guitarist of God Forbid, "but I think that it has actually done the opposite. People who might have been on the fence about what they thought of people from other races and cultures have jumped that fence, from one side to the other. If you look at the statistics on . . . white supremacist websites, they have increased in activity."

During the 2008 presidential election, Coyle wrote a column on race and politics for the popular MetalSucks.net. "I became very unpopular in a lot of metal circles because of what I was saying about John McCain and Obama," he says. "It was a risk to do it but I didn't care, because it didn't matter to me. I figured I could say anything because I'm half-black and half-white. But even then, a white guy will just label me as being black and not acknowledge my whiteness.

"I've seen YouTube comments of people who cannot believe that I'm half-black, and they will say that I'm Hispanic. They won't believe it. There are a lot of deep, psychological issues that go along within music and race, and I think that metal is the only musical style where it is really apparent."

Despite the prevailing stereotypes about metal, hardcore, and punk fans regarding class status, and despite the current resurgence in popularity of metal among the younger generation of fans, from middle-class hipsters to more people of color, there is always a group of seemingly angry men and women that are looking for a place to vent their frustration. Some of it is focused on the personal hardships they are facing. Some of it is simply just a desire to get drunk, get high, and fight. As backwards as it sounds, I wonder if some feel that a black commander in chief signifies another loss to their privilege, making the metal scene more hostile to black men and women.

In many cases of racism within the music scene, the things the artists say *outside* of their music are the most problematic. When faced with offensive lyrical content, people can simply avoid bands that openly boast of being white supremacists or anti-Semitic or homophobic, along with bands that trade in offensive and tasteless humor, like the somewhat satirical Anal Cunt, whose song titles, such as "You're Pregnant, So I Kicked You in the Stomach," give prospective listeners a strong indication of what to expect.

Revered nineteenth-century classical composer Richard Wagner was one of the first musicians to become a "catalyst for the ultimate 'art over politics' debate in music," argues Justin Davisson in his essay "Extreme Politics and Extreme Metal: Strange Bedfellows or Fellow Travelers?" in the journal *The Metal Void*. Hitler was reportedly inspired by Wagner's writing and musical compositions. So are a number of metal bands, such as Manowar and Rammstein. Wagner's music was reportedly played at Nazi events, and Hitler used it to close his radio addresses. In 1850, and initially using a pseudonym, Wagner published the essay *"Das Judenthum in der Musik"*—"Judaism in Music," which argued that Jewish musicians and artists should not be allowed in the world of art because of their "coldness and indifference, triviality and nonsense."

Despite an "unwritten ban" on Wagner's music in Israel, in 2001 composer Daniel Barenboim conducted a portion of Wagner's opera "Tristan and Isolde" at the annual Israel Festival. He did acknowledge what he was doing by inviting people who might be offended by his musical selection to leave—and many did. Barenboim asked a highly contentious question: Can you separate the musician's personal views from the music?

I wondered about those of us who consider ourselves free of prejudice or even antiracist. How do we react to offensive personal views of musicians they enjoy? Do we simply chalk everything up to free speech? What about when a person in a band I admire says something that disrespects me and my sensibilities directly?

As a black female fan who listens to music that sometimes denigrates women and minorities, I encounter multiple opportunities for outrage. I'm more offended by racist, homophobic, and anti-Semitic views than by overtly sexist remarks within music. That is, except for misogyny in hip hop, when predominantly black men are talking about black women or other women of color, which is especially hurtful, as the music is supposed to be the communal voice of both black men and women.

Heavy metal lyrics have had their problems, dating back to the infamous civil suit leveled at Judas Priest in 1990, when the band was accused of being culpable for the death of one man after two Nevada teenagers shot themselves after allegedly listening Priest's cover of Spooky Tooth's "Better by You, Better Than Me" off of 1978's *Stained Class*. At the end of the

1990s, the music of Marilyn Manson was criticized after the 1999 shootings at Columbine High School in Denver. Other bands, such as Gwar, Deicide, and Cannibal Corpse have been publicly criticized and protested against for lyrical content and album cover art.

After a couple especially sexist and misogynist blog posts popped up on metal sites during the winter of 2011, I contacted a colleague who is well versed in contemporary women's issues. Jonathan Smith is a metal journalist for Hellbound.ca and a doctoral student at Wilfrid Laurier University. He did his undergraduate degree in women's studies. "We have to be careful about casting too wide a net when it comes to representation versus reality in terms of sexism and misogyny in music," he says. "For example, the death metal band Cannibal Corpse has long received flak about how their lyrics and imagery depict violence against women. The band has explained that they are channeling other forms of art such as exploitation horror films and violent comic books. I'm uncomfortable with equating their cartoonish portrayals of violence against women with the actual, often sexualized, violence committed against women every day, not by random attackers but mostly by lovers, friends, and family."

Perhaps the sexist remarks within metal are just so over-the-top and stupid that I shouldn't take them seriously. But there is a level of pure hate in the music and the personal views of some artists that could easily serve as a catalyst for physical violence—and that makes me uncomfortable. "I've defended violent forms of art in the past when it's clear that its creators do not actually endorse the violence depicted in their work," says Smith, "and they are willing to intelligently discuss the possible social implications of such depictions. Sexual violence and misogynistic attitudes are problems within our societies in general, and definitely not limited to any one type of art or popular culture. It's a complex conversation that I hope metal communities have and will continue to have outside of their love of the music."

"I don't know if its fair to say, but for some reason, it means more to me and it can be more hurtful when it's a racial issue than when it's a gender issue," says Drexel University's Devon Powers. "I listen to all kinds of music that is sexist, totally sexist, and I'm more able to let that roll off my back and not even think about it. But if somebody says something racial, than I'd probably try to avoid the particular music. If I was thinking of buying their album or going to a show, then I just wouldn't do it."

For example, though Cannibal Corpse's lyrics are disturbing and offensive, I do not have a visceral reaction to them. I do not think that men who have a negative view of women are going to take a song like "Fucked with a Knife" seriously, because it is blatantly tongue-in-cheek. However, I understand that the real potential for violence toward women remains.

"One of my favorite singers is Elvis Costello, and there was an incident that happened in the late 1970s," Powers says, referring to a drunken hotel bar brawl in 1979 sparked by Costello calling James Brown a "jive-ass nigger" and Ray Charles a "blind nigger." "He also has a couple of songs in which he says the word 'nigger,' and he uses the word 'darkie,' and I still listen to him. I even have his autograph. I've met him a bunch of times. But I can't listen to those particular songs."

Sexism and misogyny in music are almost always protected by freedom of speech. In art, freedom of expression is a common defense against offensiveness, but the line between freedom and purposeful hate messages is uncomfortably fluid and often subjective.

In the spring of 2009, singer Philip Anselmo was invited to speak to students at Loyola University in his hometown of New Orleans. Best known as the former singer of Pantera, Anselmo is currently the singer for Down, and owner of the Housecore record label. He is known for having very strong opinions on everything from music to boxing to drug abuse. During Anselmo's appearance, despite his rough demeanor, he was very forthcoming and really focused on warning the students about pitfalls surrounding the music industry, including drug use.

Anselmo's appearance was a far cry from a speech he made onstage during a Pantera show in Montreal in 1995. I had known one of two black women that had attended this show, where the singer made a stand against what felt to us like the black community. The whole incident, while intriguing and disturbing at the time—it was even mentioned in the *Montreal Gazette* review of the concert—had totally slipped my mind for years, but of course it survives today on YouTube clip titled "Phil Anselmo Gives White Pride Speech."

Here's a portion of Anselmo's speech that night:

"I have a problem. Look, if you have read any of my lyrics, we, Pantera, have friends of many colors and many kinds. We are not a racist band. If you conduct yourself like a gentleman, and you act like a human being, you want to be treated as such. I'm going to make this short and sweet. The thing that bothers me the most is the black bands and all the fucking black kids buying their albums and shit because it sounds neat and then they go the clubs and dance to this rap shit and take Ecstasy and that shit. The rap bands—the majority of them—are pissing all over white culture. They don't want your culture at all. They're fucking dogging all white people and they don't know any of us. In the United States, where we live, black people walk around with T-shirts that say . . . 'Stop black on black crime,' which means to stop black people from killing each other. But what I say to you—it's okay to kill white people? That's what it says to me. It's okay to kill a white motherfucker, no problem?"

Despite his initial assertions that neither he nor his band is racist, in my opinion as a black woman, the vitriol in Anselmo's demeanor and his voice indicated otherwise. For me and for the women I spoke to writing this book—many of us fans of Pantera and of Anselmo in particular—"white pride" is nonetheless synonymous with racism. "White pride" is a catchphrase used by supremacists on *Dr. Phil* or *Jerry Springer* and, hell, even on the early days of *Oprah*, as to why they weren't racist. I couldn't help but feel the tone of racial bias—with blacks on the undesirable end. The audience's applause didn't help the feeling in the pit of my stomach.

Back when I first heard about Anselmo's diatribe, I tried to be optimistic. My initial thought was that he sounded pretty ignorant, but I tried to look at the subject matter from a different perspective. In 1995, there was a swell of gangsta rap groups, and some, including N.W.A and Onyx, were quite militant in their views. As a former hip hop head, I didn't remember any of them overtly promoting killing white people.

The most militant messages weren't from hip hop, anyway, but from Ice-T's metal band. In 1992, Body Count's first album, *Cop Killer*, aroused the ire of Vice President Dan Quayle, who called it "obscene." Protests of the record label by policemen eventually led to the removal of the single "Cop Killer" from the album. However, Ice-T insisted that the track was a first-person narrative about wanting to kill a police officer for revenge—not specifically a white one.

I would agree that the song was popular among my friends and me because it was directed toward the perceived injustice that many felt about those in authority. We wanted retribution for those who had been victimized, not to kill based on skin color. Regardless, many cultural theorists feel that the majority of people who are buying hip hop albums today are actually white, suburban males drawn to the music production, who want to live vicariously though the angst-filled lyrics. At that time, black communities in urban populations did have a tenuous relationship with authority figures. In 1991, the brutal beating that Rodney King received from Los Angeles police officers set people on edge. So yes, some young black folks were angry, and some of those frustrations were translated though the music of that era. But Anselmo's theory about rap groups encouraging blacks to kill white people simply wasn't true. Stopping black-on-black crime does not mean starting black-on-white crime; that just doesn't make sense.

While his argument wasn't quite fleshed out, Anselmo was partially correct about a rise in black awareness. Thanks partly to the growing popularity of rap music, the 1980s spawned a resurgence of black pride that had been temporarily abandoned. Black folks were buying novels by Alice Walker and Toni Morrison; rediscovering the works of Ralph Ellison, Langston Hughes, and James Baldwin; fawning over movies by Spike Lee. Perhaps because of his film, *Malcolm X*, people reconsidered the beliefs of the black activist again, who had been hitherto deemed an angry and hateful militant, in contrast with the beloved Martin Luther King.

We started using popular slogans, such as "Too Black, Too Strong," in an attempt to send a message to the outside world that we were no longer trying to deny or be ashamed of our blackness. We were tired of trying to accommodate a society that we realized would never really accept us unless we conformed to its mores. To me, the "white culture" part of Anselmo's speech was indicative of a belief that white culture was something everyone in America should adhere to. The age-old problem remains that even when black people try to fit into white society, we are still racially stereotyped. Why try and join a club where you are not wanted?

The slogan "It's a black thing, you wouldn't understand," symbolized the frustration that black folks had with always trying to explain why they were angry and disheartened. We were sick of trying to explain the hidden aspects of racism, such as institutional and systemic issues that affected processes as simple as getting an apartment or a job.

It's difficult to explain the everyday nuances, like being followed around a store or having someone snatch their purse away from you on the street like you were going to jack them. It's tiring to try and explain to white friends or even family members the everyday frustrations that you experience, because unless they've walked in your shoes, they'll never really understand.

Quite frankly, what Anselmo and a number of metal bands either forget or simply do not acknowledge is that not everybody in the audience looks like them. In some ways, to assume that they do is natural, as the metal, hardcore, and punk scenes primarily consist of white men. But if the members of metal bands can consist of men and women from various ethnicities and cultures, why wouldn't the listeners? After all, to want to dedicate yourself to a music scene and lifestyle that most often means you are not going to make a lot of money, most likely you have to have been an ardent fan, drawn by some deeper compulsion to the sound.

The two young black women at that 1995 show were ardent Pantera fans, and the *Montreal Gazette* reported on their confrontation with Anselmo after they found their way backstage that night after the show. An article in the *Montreal Gazette* under the headline "Pantera Singer Apologizes for Racist Tirade" detailed their confrontation with Anselmo, noted that their dismay had turned them off the band, and also quoted from a letter of apology written after Anselmo had left Canada.

"I must take responsibility for the harmful words that may have racially offended our audience," Anselmo wrote. "First, to the black girl who has seen Pantera six times, thank you for telling me how upset you were at me; it made a difference and I was very sincere with my apology. Second, I'd once again like to apologize to the security guards at the show. They were classy and professional, and came to talk to me after the show when they really didn't need to at all. They opened my eyes. And yes, they were black men. I have much respect for them. I extend my apologies and a thank-you to them."

The *Gazette* continued: "Anselmo's explanation for his speech was that he was 'reacting angrily to something that recently happened in my life to someone very close to me.'"

I still wonder about the effects of his tirade that night. Not so much because of what he said, but the way he said it, and to whom. In the context of a reasoned debate, he might have had some valid points buried in there somewhere. There are questions to be asked about the popularity of the more racially charged subspecies of hip hop among white kids. The reasons could range from youthful rebellion, fashion, guilt, agreement with black anger, to just the overpowering groove. But delivering this particular speech in the context of an intense, visceral performance, where the interaction between the artist and the audience is a reflex of physical energy and rage, Anselmo seemed to be less an outspoken rebel and more like an archetype of an angry redneck.

After that night, and following similar comments in other cities during that tour, Pantera alienated black fans and white antiracist allies. However, based on the comments about Anselmo from that time that still linger on right-wing hate sites, he was celebrated by white supremacist groups. Fast-forward almost twenty years. This nearly forgotten incident has been revived by the continued existence of the YouTube clips documenting the tirade. Many viewers clearly adhere to the "white pride" portion of Anselmo's sentiments.

I was a huge Pantera fan in the 1990s. I saw the band perform a few times, and, remarkably, I have several black friends and acquaintances who don't consider themselves fans of metal but loved Pantera. The band's southern-fried groove reminded them of black-centric musical styles; whether Pantera were a metal band or not, the deep blues foundation of their later albums made black folks want to *get down*. On the flip side, rumors about Anselmo's public comments concerning race confirmed the worst suspicions of blacks who assume that the whole metal genre is riddled with racists. Black women metal fans and musicians for whom Pantera served as an introduction to heavy music wanted to know what was up.

Straight Line Stitch's Alexis Brown was turned on to metal by her older brother, and Pantera was one of the first bands she loved. "When I heard those rumors, I was like, 'What, are you serious?' Everybody loves Pantera. But it really turned me off."

Erika Kristen admits that she chose not to support Pantera because of the rumors about Anselmo, but changed her mind years later when she attended the Milwaukee Metalfest and was impressed with Anselmo's response when a group of skinheads entered the mosh pit during his set with his band

Down. "I remember thinking, 'I'm going up to the rafters because I don't want to be in that pit. They are going to fucking kill me. They are going to see my little ass and want to bring me in and stomp me down.' But there was some goose-stepping in the pit, and Phil himself stopped everything and he said, 'You know what? I will come off this stage and beat your fucking ass. You need to stop what you're doing. You're not welcome here. I don't even know where you get this shit.' Sure enough, the security guards came down and took them out."

Furthermore, Kristen felt very welcome in the presence of Down guitarist Kirk Windstein, a Louisiana-based musician like his bandmate Anselmo. "Unfortunately, Phil cannot live down some things," she says. "Kirk Windstein is the most beautiful man on the planet. For him to sit there and want to share a drink with us and to get to know us on a real level—us being black chicks in this scene—he gave us respect. And he even spoke up for Phil, and told us, 'You know what? He's a lovable guy and fans will take what they will. It is up to people who know how to stand up, speak up, and speak against it.'"

Usually when faced with bias claims, metal musicians commonly repeat a cliché like: "I'm not prejudiced, I hate everybody equally." Phil Anselmo was not the first musician to behave inappropriately in the public sphere; neither was Elvis Costello. A current strain of metal, however, does propagate unapologetic racism.

In the spring of 2010, Varg Vikernes prepared to release his first Burzum album after spending almost sixteen years in a Norwegian prison. Vikernes was convicted of murdering a friend and bandmate, Øystein Aarseth, aka Euronymous of Mayhem, and also of burning four historic churches. Vikernes has been very open regarding his disdain for visible minorities, Jews, and homosexuals, both before his incarceration and after. In a 2010 interview for Sterogum.com, he said: "I am a narrow-minded ultra-conservative anti-religious misanthropic and arrogant bigot, alright, and I have a problem with just about everything and everyone in this world, but

I am not demented. If those who are not like me are able to enjoy my music that is all fine by me. Be a Christian-born black gay feminist converted to Judaism for all I care, or worse; a Muslim. Just stay off my lawn."

I do not enjoy the music. To mark the occasion of a new Burzum release, *Decibel* magazine put Vikernes on its cover. Though a rabid fan of the magazine, I chose not to purchase the issue. The following month, the editors pointedly acknowledged the controversy their cover had generated. Some letters from readers veered toward the "Okay he's got some offensive views, but his music is great," perspective, dismissing those who opposed that sentiment as being "liberal," in this case meaning "too sensitive."

In December 2008, I went down to Atlanta to interview two black women involved the city's hardcore scene. Atlanta was interesting. Though I spent only a very brief time there, it seemed to me that this predominantly African-American city was a natural setting for blacks to be involved in whatever music scene was happening at the moment. A white crust punker with a full mouth of rotten teeth told me how white musicians in the city's punk and hardcore scene socialized with hip hop artists, bonding over excessive drugs and drinking, if not the music they performed. I chatted with some locals, including Darren Sanders, brother of Mastodon bassist Troy Sanders, and all-around roadie for the band. He mentioned an upcoming free concert that was not yet announced, and encouraged me to head back to Atlanta for the show.

A few weeks later, the Scion Rock Fest 2009 was revealed to the public, immediately followed by controversy about one band on the roster. The Chicago-based Nachtmystium was kicked off the lineup, because early in their career they had ties to distributors that traded in right-wing "national socialist black metal," or NSBM. While Nachtmystium commenced to demonstrate that the ties were tenuous or didn't exist, even loose affiliations with outfits with Nazi leanings were more than enough to make Scion organizers and many concert attendees queasy.

The Southern Poverty Law Center reported on one early Nachtmystium contact, Vinland Winds: "A newspaper reporter once asked the owner of Vinland Winds, a man who identifies himself as 'Grimnir Wotansvolk,' to explain his vision for the future. 'Easy,' Grimnir replied. 'We would export all the niggers, Jews, and newspaper reporters back to a little town called Tel Aviv, where they would be forced to toss Ariel Sharon's salad.'"

Nachtmystium's music has been described as "psychedelic black metal," influenced by Killing Joke, Joy Division, Pink Floyd, and black metal acts like Darkthrone and Burzum. The band may have been a victim of circumstance, as spiraling nihilism in the early-2000s black metal scene led to a brief surge in fascination with the so-called NSBM. The questionable religious and political beliefs of black metal were twisted and distorted into a small but global sub-subgenre of heavy metal that praised paganism, fascism and Nazism. Following their Scion scare, Nachtmystium issued a press release, refuting any claim that they were racists. The band has since prospered, and moved on to legitimate and more prestigious metal labels.

"I would not spend money on them and I refuse to see them live after I found out they were once on a label that had a nationalistic background," says Chicago-based journalist Keidra Chaney. "But at the same time, they play with bands that I know don't share their beliefs. And it's hard to be a person of color, because I have friends who ask, 'Are you going?' and I say, 'I'm not going, because I'm not spending my money on them.'"

I distributed a questionnaire to black women while researching this book, asking about their attitudes toward racism and entertainers. A sizable two-fifths of respondents said that they would immediately boycott an artist if they found out he or she held racist views or made a racist comment in public. An equal two-fifths said that they would likely lose respect for the performer, but wouldn't let that get in the way of enjoying the music. The remaining one-fifth said that knowing a performer was openly racist wouldn't deter them at all.

"I would try to learn more about the incident," explained one person I contacted. "If the person does turn out to be racist, I could not enjoy their music any longer and I would get rid of it."

"I would evaluate the situation, overall," another woman replied. "After finding out Axl Rose dropped an n-bomb in a song, I lost respect for him as a person, but that doesn't change the importance of their music. In hip hop artists make racist, sexist, homophobic commentary all the time."

"There are too many exceptions to have a simple black-and-white answer," adds Chaney. "I think for any metal fan of color, it is an individual choice. It's my decision to not pay money to see Nachtmystium. I would say to my black or minority friends who want to go see them, 'Word.' But that's just me."

But do white folks even realize or care when a band or artist holds racist views? Jason Netherton, vocalist and bassist for Misery Index, believes that for metal fans the music is more important than the musician. "I think that if there is a great musician and they put out great records then if they are black it's not going to matter to the metal fans. It might have in the early days, but I think that things have really leveled out."

"I strongly believe that fans *do care* when a band holds negative views about people of color," says Kristen. "However, what happens if it doesn't directly affect them? Will they speak up about it? I don't really know. When it comes to someone falling in the mosh pit, somebody is supposed to help them up. It's supposed to be a community and it usually transcends any color. But I do think that the majority of fans are really ignorant. They just don't know, and there is ignorance in simply not knowing that there is a problem out there, and that there are people who are uncomfortable."

"I happen to have the worst friends on the planet," laughs Monique Craft, a hardcore and metal fan. "One of my really good friends will be the first person to call a black person a 'nigger' if they step out of place with him. Another best friend of mine, and she's like a sister to me, but once someone stole her cell and the first thing that came out of her mouth was, 'Some fucking nigger stole my phone.' I was like, 'Jesus Christ! I'm standing right in front of you.'" I know they are not racist, I know that they are just ignorant, and they would be the first to punch someone out if they came up to me and called me a nigger."

I was drawn to bands like Misery Index and Dying Fetus because they communicate important social commentary via intense grindcore-influenced death metal. When artists promote social and political messages, the responses are mixed, to say the least. "Fans like the music, the energy, and the anger, and definitely the lyrics come second, if not last, for a lot of people," notes Netherton. "It's unfortunate, but I don't think that people would appreciate more socially conscious lyrics or lyrics that are critical of racism or homophobia. I tend to find that the more blatant you are with your message, the reaction or response you will get is more critical."

In terms of bands in which members hold staunch political or religious beliefs, most metal fans know what they are getting into. The fans vote with their wallets. And a journalist and photographer like Kristen votes with her pen and her camera. "There are a couple of black metal bands out there that when they come through Chicago, we don't support them," she says. "What better way to get them where it hurts than in their pockets? We don't give them any press. We don't even talk about them, and we encourage other journalists not to talk about them. You don't put light on those people, and don't give them the money."

In some ways, the metal scene deserves some credit, because at least its racism is worn on its sleeve, misguidedly proclaimed from the stage or in interviews in an attempt at honesty. "A lot of people of color believe that there is something good within these people," admits Kristen. "We met Dimebag Darrell from Pantera, God rest his soul, right before he died. He was cool as hell. He is from the South, and in that backstage area he was flying a Confederate flag. Do they believe in it? Absolutely. But as we were passing through, he was kind to us. 'Hey, do you want a smoke? Do you want to party?' Sure!"

If we as consumers really knew even what the guy who owns the convenience store down the street thinks about race, we might be unpleasantly surprised. "As a woman, maybe you shouldn't listen to any kind of metal," says Chaney. "I was looking through *Guitar World* today, and that is a sexist magazine, but I'm not going to stop buying it, because I fucking play an instrument. It gets to be ridiculous at a point. Unless I'm only going to pay money for *Girls Playing Guitar* magazine, at some point I have to make a decision."

"The negativity will stick around, but there need to be more people who will find the good in people, and folks that are out there to shed the light on it," adds Kristen. "We need a lot of people out there to shine a light on racism and to educate people. Education is power. I know that sounds like a public service announcement, but that's the truth."

A black woman who attends a concert is most likely just as dedicated as the white man or woman standing beside her. But in the dim lights of the club or theater, racist patrons often seize the moment to unload their thoughts about the entire black community. I spoke to a stunningly beautiful twenty-something with impeccable style, total confidence, and a fearlessness that almost scared me, and she told me about getting punched in the face by a skinhead at a show. After ignoring a warning to stay out of the mosh pit, she went back in and ended up being chased by men. Luckily, some of the guys who worked at the club came to her rescue. She brushed off my look of surprise with a shrug. "It's part of the game."

But I think race-based verbal abuse and physical assault against anyone is a serious offense, and should have no place wherever people gather to enjoy music. What is particularly disturbing is that these attacks nullify any "gender pass" a woman might ordinarily get within a predominantly male environment. I'm talking about violence directed toward black women because we are black in an environment in where we aren't wanted.

My nonblack female colleagues in the scene recall few, if any, instances of unprovoked violent verbal and physical altercations. They have experienced sexual harassment, but for the most part, men are exceedingly polite to them, even moving to make sure a woman can see the stage if she happens to be standing amongst men who are taller than she. Sure, it can seem patronizing and a little silly to treat a woman at a death metal show as particularly fragile. But any day of the week that beats being screamed at or hit without provocation.

The violence that others and myself have experienced leads me to observe that racism erodes our humanity. When I am coded as an "other" in the scene, those negative reactions degrade my human right to be respected not only as a woman, but as a person. It is extremely scary for me to be regarded by someone as so utterly worthless, especially in an environment in which they feel their actions meet with little—if any—repercussion. (And for the most part, they are right.)

When she was younger, Michelle Lane-Ogden was heavily involved in the goth music scene. She described to me how she inadvertently walked into a concert where the opening band included skinheads. "My husband was celebrating his fortieth birthday. No one else seemed to have a problem with them being there, and since the promoters booked them, I'm guessing the owners of this establishment had no problem with them being there, either."

She describes people averting their eyes from her during the show. "Each time I made my way to the bathroom, or went to order a drink, people looked at me. As soon as I tried to connect, they looked away, as if to say, 'What's she doing here?' I've dealt with exclusion and feeling invisible my entire life, but this was ridiculous. Why should these attitudes be acceptable in the alternative music scene?" She was no greenhorn, either, having grown up "in areas of Pennsylvania that are notorious for hate groups, including Nazi skinheads."

Pisso, a former skinhead herself, recalls an episode that took place when she attended a punk show in Wisconsin. "I tried to suppress this incident because it depressed me. There was this one band that were inviting people on the stage, and they asked all the girls to come up. I get up on the stage and we were singing along to some song. Then the next song was called 'Let Your Tits Hang Out,' and I was like 'fuck this,' and left the stage. I do listen to some bands that have some raunchy songs, but in this situation I wasn't going to stand onstage whey they sang that song.

"I went to get off the stage and the singer made this comment about me, because I did have, like, a skin girl haircut. He said, 'Oh, is this the future of skinheads?' and he gestured toward me in a very negative way. It definitely made me think about the scene and my place in it. I have encountered older skinheads from England or older guys in the scene where I felt that there was some racism. Even though I know a lot about the skinhead movement, I have read interviews with older bands and they'll say 'Oh, we're not racist, but whites are whites and blacks are blacks, and they are different, and don't like hanging out together.' It's depressing."

One of the most difficult things to explain is, even when no one has verbally or physically assaulted you, the tension in the air can be just painful to endure. "I think that black kids are smart enough—I think that they can feel it," says Dallas Coyle. "Sometimes you can feel the tension more than someone saying something,"

Some will call it paranoia, but in North American society, where there are more instances where black women will be in spaces where they are the minority, such as at a corporation or a university, that visceral sense of tension is a familiar feeling. "There are moments in life where you think to yourself, 'And this is why race still matters. And this is why I feel different," says Powers. "If I'm at an indie rock show and I'm the only black person there and if nobody says anything to me, it still feels weird. It's never *just* music, which is why I think that the lyrics included in the songs are articulations of identity and ways of positioning yourself in the world. As consumer[s] and fan[s], black women are using music as a way to interface a sense of themselves with a sense of other people and how [they] situate [themselves] in the world."

When Monique Craft lived near Pittsburgh, she had physical run-ins with skinheads at hardcore shows. "I've been hit a couple of times, and that's been super-scary. I try and be as brave as possible and not think about it, just overcome it and forget about it."

She recalls one incident that made my blood run cold. "I was at a show and this smaller girl who had a buzz haircut walked into me and spilled my drink. And I was like, 'Hey, douche bag, you spilled my drink. Are you going to buy me a new one?' So this girl gets into my face and starts calling me names and we get into it. She almost, *almost* said 'nigger' but not quite. She caught herself, but I was flipping out on her. Then her boyfriend came up and completely backed her up. 'Nigger' started flowing and flowing, and then a punch came out of left field. I had no idea what happened. I just went down on the ground and blacked out. When I came to, I saw friends of mine who were fighting the guy, and for a second, I didn't even know what happened. Things got broken up really quickly—they never last too long at those shows—and I just carried on with my night. I was a little paranoid when I left the show, but I have learned to get over things like that really quickly, so I don't have any emotions over that incident. It sucked that it happened, but it never worries me, because I know I have many people in my life who don't feel that way."

Despite the commonsense approach that all public spaces are for everyone, Pisso observes that the hardcore scene is commonly thought to be a space where white men feel they can escape from the outside world. "It's all about male bonding. I have a white male friend in Oakland [who] complains that it's hard for him to get a job. He feels that sometimes he is seen as the enemy, like there are already so many white men in power that people would rather choose a black woman or a person who is disabled over him. I can appreciate that he feels he can actually talk to me about that, but guys like him go to these shows feeling like they have to be amongst themselves, in an environment where they don't have to worry about women or minorities or anything [like] that."

Probably the most troubling facet of discussing racism in the metal, hardcore, and punk scenes is that the people who are most affected by racism are the ones criticized for bringing up the issue. Black women fans have a difficult time in sharing their stories with their nonblack friends, because they fear that their concerns will not be believed or, even worse, that they'll be dismissed. When I was at leaving the Kyuss Lives! show, I wondered if the people who were staring at me (and not at the guy who called me a nigger) would have intervened if I were physically attacked. The vibe I got in the room was that they would not have helped me.

The most important thing is feeling that the people that you attend shows with are willing to support you. "I have had enough friends in the scene who are aware and who do support me," says Pisso. "And if somebody said something to me at a show, they would have my back. It's a balanced experience. I do meet people who are in the scene who would still be shocked at what I've experienced."

Powers says that the ability to not feel or care about racism is an example of white privilege. "It's uncomfortable to talk about race," she says, "especially in the American context. It is especially fraught with tension. Although it has become more kosher to say racially motivated stuff in public, especially among white liberals the worst thing is to be branded a racist. Anything that smacks of that, especially an insensitivity [regarding] the experience of a person of color, it's like they can't imagine anything worse—'Oh no, I'm one of *those* people.' It becomes very personal as, people don't like to confront their own racial bias[es]."

A couple years ago I wrote a concert review on my own blog, *Writing Is Fighting*, and mentioned a rumor that was told to me about a member of one of the bands. I thought nothing of it after the fact, as I tried to make it as innocuous as possible—no finger pointing; I didn't even name the band. I did write that I would no longer consider buying an album from that band.

My choice. My blog. However, a couple of months later, I got a phone call from someone who had been contacted by someone in the band's camp who read my blog post and put two and two together. The caller said that there would be legal action if I didn't pull the post down. At first I protested, but I decided to do it, as I had a feeling that if I didn't there would be trouble all around.

When I went in to remove the post, however, I saw that someone had already recently commented. Here is a bit of what they said:

"For you to accuse completely innocent people (which they are, 100% for sure) and their dead relatives of such atrocities and crimes against humanity is truly malicious, and on top of that it is just furthering the divide and nurturing the intolerance and ignorance that permeate this society in general. You're assuming a dangerously great deal, and your words carry more weight than you may realize. Think about what you're potentially doing to these innocent guys and their fledgling music career. All because some idiot told you something that wasn't true? Solid."

I replied at length, and, admittedly, the further I got along in my response, the angrier I got. "I think that you are more pissed that it was actually brought up, rather than the actual accusation," I wrote at one point. "Do not turn this around and try to make me the guilty party because you read something you didn't like."

In hindsight, I wasn't sure that I should have pulled the post, and I likely shouldn't have mentioned the rumor in the first place. But whether the story I heard was true or not, I was writing about my reaction to hearing allegations of a racist past. If the story wasn't true, I could have sullied the band's reputation, and I would have felt pretty awful about that.

But would it really sully their reputation? Would fans of a band with a racist skeleton in the closet cry and create a bonfire, tossing their albums into the flames? I honestly do not think so. One thing that I have observed in discussions about race is that it is difficult to coax an active response from anyone not in a marginalized group themselves. Maybe this is natural—if everyone was compelled to action because of social injustice, we would have few problems in the world. We tend to spring into action only when an action or an insult affects us personally. We are a society that wants to avoid issues that promise us no tangible results and no tangible rewards should we engage them.

I went to Texas in March 2010 for the South by Southwest (SXSW) music and film festival. One evening I went to meet some friends at a show by the same band I'd talked about on my blog. I arrived just as the band finished their set and the club was about to close for the night. As I entered, throngs of people were exiting. One guy, a skinhead, saw me, sneered at me, and body-slammed me into a wall. I didn't fall, or I would have been trampled, and I wasn't hurt, but I was shaken up. I couldn't help wondering again about the damning story I had been told, and I couldn't help judging the band by the audience they attracted.

So, you might ask, why do black women keep on attending shows and, more than that, why do I actively participate in the metal scene? Because it is my right to do so. One of most satisfying things I realized after interviewing women for this book is that we all share the same attitude. Come hell or high water, none of us will ever back down from a fight.

VIII. Remove the Barricades— and Stage Dive!

"Does anyone know of any magazine editors of urban magazines who would be willing to talk about black rock artists? Hit me up, please" —@lainad

"@lainad: Magazine editors [ha!] of urban magazines [ha! ha!] willing to talk about black rock artists [hahahahahahahahaha *has stroke, dies*]" —@pdfreeman

I HAVE TO AGREE WITH MY FRIEND PHIL. After a fruitless decade of pitching black-centric magazines stories on individual black rock artists, and investigative features on blacks in the metal scene, I already knew the answer to my question before I asked. The interest level was so low that one of the best responses I can remember would be an actual reply stating "No, thanks." I was hoping somebody else out there had a better experience. If these publications were covering black hockey players, black golf stars, and essentially every other black celebrity who has conquered a sport or profession in which black folks had historically been scarce, why not a nod to black metal, punk, and hardcore artists?

Fortunately, getting a diverse range of music to the masses is now easier than it has ever been. We are no longer reliant on mainstream radio, television, or print publications to dictate what we should or shouldn't listen to. That's lucky, because social segregation based on race and class play a bigger part than ever in how music is marketed through those channels. With the industry in rapid declining, marketers are more focused than ever on promoting easily packaged artists that have a hope of a profitable return. The music industry caters to the general population's trends and preferences. It's a special thing when labels have taken risks on alternative artists who, because of their unique appearance or other attributes, at first might not appear to fit into a mold, but have gone on to have success. Present-day metal, hardcore, and punk music is more often based on a do-it-yourself ethic, which makes creating music, distributing, and touring much harder than doing so under the auspices of a major label, but at least the musicians control their own sounds and images. Money is scarce, but throughout the underground music scene, there is a general awareness of the financial struggles among the bands. Even fans and media understand these realities.

Established bands, such as Metallica, Megadeth, Slayer, Slipknot, Iron Maiden, and even relative newcomers like Mastodon have been able to maintain full-time careers on major labels and generate Grammy nominations and other hallmarks of mainstream success. All these bands changed the rules of the music business in different ways, and they all began on small, independent labels. Today, there are more independent labels than ever before that specifically cater to extreme musical genres, and they take risks with their budgets for advertising, recording, and tour support.

"I don't think there is any question that metal labels offer a lot more opportunities for bands with minority and/or female members," says Scott Alisoglu, whose company, Clawhammer PR, works with metal, punk, rock, and hardcore artists. "The vast majority of metal fans couldn't care less about race or gender, even if the fans might not be the most progressive people. Even females fronting metal bands has not been such a big deal the past several years, as most metal fans just want to know whether the goods can be delivered."'

Smaller labels have a closer connection to the music, and the people who run them are usually more interested in catering to music fans. Depending on how these label heads consider the implications surrounding race and gender in the scene, I feel optimistic about opportunities for black female musicians to get a break. All it would take is one runaway success by a black woman musician on one of these indie labels to open the doors wide, and possibly change the way even the mainstream music industry decides who to sign and who to turn away.

Thirty years ago, FM radio stations were prime movers in the decision-making processes of young music buyers. Radio stations printed their top-ten lists in the newspapers; they let you know what was cool music to listen to and what was not. Many people don't remember how powerfully radio enforced racial segregation. That legacy of racial segregation on the airwaves, beginning with the shunning of black artists in favor of white artists performing black-centric music and leading to ultraprecise programming formats today, remains a major contributor to the racial divide in popular music.

In Darrell M. McNeill's essay "Rock, Racism, and Retailing 101," the cofounder of the Black Rock Coalition defines "race music" as a category used by marketers to describe all black musical artists, regardless of musical genre. According to McNeill, when the Great Depression began in 1929, the entire record industry, after selling about $100 million of records in the mid-1920s, cut back on the number of records being produced. Certain categories suffered—no folk or hillbilly and no race records were created or sold for three years. That ruled out work for any black artists. That neglect created opportunity, however, as performing rights organization Broadcast Music, Inc., or BMI, formed as a lower-cost alternative to the dominant ASCAP. BMI helped disenfranchised radio stations stay on the air by offering cheaper licensing fees for such disparate categories of music as folk, hillbilly, and race music.

Fast forward to the postwar 1940s. A migration of southern blacks to northern states brought people access to more forms of music that they had never heard before. Americans also had money again. Race music became somewhat popular, though it was mostly played late at night. Eventually, in the form of rhythm and blues, or R&B, black music was finally deemed acceptable for regular radio listeners.

White labels soon created black music divisions, which competed with a plethora of black-owned record labels that prospered in the post–World War II economic boom. These white labels saw the profits and the appeal of black music, and sought a way to channel that energy from the relative obscurity of race music and into popular music proper. Sam Phillips, owner of Sun Records, opined that white people would prefer to listen to this new style of music if the person singing it was white. White musicians like Bill Haley and the Comets and, soon after, Elvis Presley emerged, playing rock 'n' roll in a form that was palatable to white audiences.

But black radio didn't help either, as station formats guided audience taste, leading black listeners to make a distinction about what music was acceptable for them, and what music was not. Soul music first appeared in Chicago's R&B scene in the early 1960s. A fusion of R&B and gospel, soul music was more rooted in the modern experiences of blacks than was the old-time blues music that dated back to the slave era. Funk music, widespread in the 1970s but pioneered earlier by artists such as James Brown, brought the guitar back to the forefront. Soon, both soul and funk, partly because of the era, were injecting political and social politics into their lyricism.

Even as this parallel black media prospered, a class divide kept up barriers to black music. Funk was the hardest music to get played on black radio. "Some people say that funk is rock music for black people," says Maureen Mahon, author of *Right to Rock*. "That's what happened to rock 'n' roll in the 1970s for blacks. But you will find that mainstream black journalism or scholarship talking about funk would present it differently, with a different trajectory. They wouldn't want to link it to rock."

"Black radio stations would play Queen's 'Another One Bites the Dust' because it had that funky bass line," says journalist Keidra Chaney. "But hardcore band Bad Brains were not seen as musically commercially viable. No one wanted to hear it. And that blows, but that's an issue of discrimination in the music industry."

Despite opening for Black Sabbath, Ted Nugent, and the Who and impressing peers like AC/DC's Angus Young with their live performances, Mother's Finest, led by singer Joyce Kennedy, had a difficult time getting airplay. Their 1992 album *Black Radio Won't Play This Record* featured the lead single "Like a Negro." They were correct: Black radio did not touch their record.

For a long time, a divide existed between studio music concocted for the radio, and live music played nightly by performing bands. Rock and funk fans were more likely check out a band to discover new musicians and new music. Perhaps the overproduction of R&B music on heavy rotation meant that people who paid to see a funk or rock performer live were disappointed because the music didn't sound as pristine as what they heard on the radio. Black audiences became reluctant to shell out money to see a performance in which there no guarantee of quality. And they missed out on a lot of great bands, especially rock and metal bands.

While certain bands might not have met the standards of a particular radio station, that in no way meant they lacked in talent. "The Roots don't sound like what is on radio," says Tamar-kali, "and that's because they have live instruments. That's what happens when young people don't see live bands. When I was a kid I never saw these bands play live, but I didn't need to, because there wasn't as much studio programming and editing to the music. I was hearing the quality in what was played on the radio. Today, people don't even sound fucking human. Look at Lil Wayne right now. It's like when you have soda pop for so long and you think that's sugar. You don't realize it when it's real—and it's that real stuff that we're lacking."

I have noticed that, when attending shows by the Roots, Living Colour, Fishbone, Rage Against the Machine, Willis Earl Beal, and Alabama Shakes, despite the black and brown folks on stage, the audiences are at least 90 percent white men. Black folks are missing the opportunity to see artists who cross musical genres and redefine what a rock band should look like. The thing that drove me crazy was the white folks at some of those shows who gave me and my friends strange looks, as though they were surprised at our attendance—they could accept black performers but didn't want us standing next to them in the crowd.

Conversely, black people have no problem attending a concert by a white rapper like Eminem. "The part of it that is significant is the creative freedom level," says Mahon. "I think white artists performing black music is perceived as okay, even though some people will take issue with it because not all the artists are great, but the music industry will accept it because white artists make more money."

Live appearances of musicians aired on television from the start of the TV era. Music videos were produced as early as 1974, and the first national music video station, MTV, played its first video in 1981. Obviously popular culture played an integral part in promoting new artists, and the visual imagery also played a huge factor. The financial stakes were higher, however, for both the television stations and the record labels producing videos, and stereotypes were equally difficult to overcome with the interjection of the visual medium into popular music. A terrifically talented and headstrong artist like Prince prospered. Many other extremely gifted black rock musicians did not.

"There are assumptions made about what mainstream black audiences will listen to," adds Mahon, "and those assumptions drive the decisions at black radio stations. Any kind of social commentary at any point in the 1970s really wasn't packaged. Party music was perceived as better—love songs, dance songs, or silly songs, what have you. You would have an occasional Stevie Wonder moment or something like that, but, generally speaking, there was not a lot of social commentary in the music."

And yet, when the divisions are breached, mass media can become responsible for black musicians and fans discovering and embracing genres of music outside of R&B and hip hop. "Nowadays, it's about the industry having its hooks in the play format," says Tamar-kali. "In the 1970s, it was more about the music. Queen was played and we loved it—if the song was good, that's all it took. I wanted a boom box but my dad wouldn't give one to me. He gave me this combo record player–radio thing, and he took one of his old leather belts and made a strap for it. So I used to carry that thing around! The radio player only had AM, so from listening to AM radio, I was exposed to a lot of great music."

Though black radio stations and black record labels put tight restrictions on the kind of music their black artists could play, virtually shutting out black hard rock and heavy metal artists altogether, all was fair game for black artists who had gotten approval from white listeners. After proving themselves commercially with hits, several black artists could not resist the urge to play heavier music. Canadian rapper Michie Mee parlayed midlevel success and a guest appearance on Queen Latifah's 1989 single "Ladies First" into the short-lived metal/reggae band Raggadeath, who released the popular single "One Life" in 1995.

In 2010, multiplatinum rapper Lil Wayne released a rock album, *Rebirth*, though it was hardly a success. "Wayne's big problem is that he seems to like the *idea* of rock music more than any actual rock music itself," wrote the *Village Voice*.

From the slave hollers used to transmit information, to the blues music that was the one art form via which black women and men could talk about the human emotions that were usually either ignored or silenced, music has always been one of the most important mechanisms for transmitting stories about black life in America. There is an unspoken bond between the music and the listener, a silent understanding that, despite their physical location, age, or gender, when musicians write about their experiences, they are shared by many people who look like them.

For black musicians in the metal, hardcore, and punk scenes, the music that they perform can seem totally alien to the black experience in America. When expressing universal emotions like love, hate, rage, and lust, there is little to differentiate black artists from white ones. "There is definitely is a tension between black folks and rock," says Judas Priestess vocalist Militia Vox. "I kind of equate it to that thing where if you are black, the lighter you are, the more you have to prove that you're black. When I started singing professionally, I felt that I had to be very militant in the way I dressed and the way I spoke, because I felt that I had something to prove. I'm still trying to prove myself for validation in other people's eyes as a woman and being black in the metal scene. People try to test me, ask me what I listen to and question how much I know about metal music. I'm like, 'C'mon man, I do the same things that you do.' I don't claim to be a metal historian, but I know what I like. I live it, I sing it, and I play it."

Berklee professor Kudisan Kai says her voice students are realists, and typically focus on musical genres in which they are almost guaranteed to find jobs after graduation. "They feel they can make a living doing certain styles of music," she says. "There is lots of music on the radio, and when a certain genre is popular, everybody wants to be a part of it. The record industry doesn't think that the masses would be interested in black female rock and alternative musicians, so they don't market it. First, how do you market women? And then black women? They just didn't know how.

"On the other hand, I think that if someone had something—whatever that 'something' is, whether it is rock music—regardless of color, it would hit," she adds. "We have come to a point in the world where we should have evolved from the past. The music industry is always looking for the 'next big thing' anyway, but because of what is happening economically, they are not taking that much of a chance."

Vox agrees: "I had one record label tell me that they were going to make me the next Lenny Kravitz, but that was not what I'm about. I was insulted. How can you look at me like that? I think that it's obvious what I'm about. A lot of the industries have their own formulas as to what they feel will work and what will not."

One allure of metal to musicians, labels, and listeners alike should be its long-term nature. The key to metal's longevity has been the devotion of fans, and anyone who has won the hearts of metal fans will own them forever (just ask openly gay metal legend Rob Halford of Judas Priest). "Metal fans are always devoted, and they love their bands, says Vox. "They buy the shirts. They want the shirts with the concert dates on them so they can tell people they were there. No other crowd or scene even gives a shit. Do you ever see anyone walking around with a Busta Rhymes concert T-shirt? You don't see that because people don't care!"

Even as more women musicians are coming to the scene, as in every other aspect of the music industry, sexism remains an issue. For black women who are drawn for whatever reasons to extreme musical genres, the challenge seems to be even more difficult. There are so few examples, that I will draw on some stories from pop punk and alternative rock. "The problem is getting equal representation within labels and amongst people who have the power to let black artists forge their own careers, both artistically and economically," says the BRC's LaRonda Davis. "We find that it does not happen that often. Singer Graph Nobel should get all the same shots that Gwen Stefani gets. We know that it doesn't happen. You can play them in a blind test and people would not know the difference, given all that we know. It doesn't happen that way. So the question still remains, why not?"

Nobel, along with fellow Canadian Fefe Dobson and Philadelphia's Res, are good examples of the record industry ignoring blatant talent—and of what happens to black female musicians whose music choices do not fit into rigid radio formats. Nobel is a fiercely determined singer from Toronto with a solid underground following. When I met her in 2004, she was broke, even though she had recently landed the cover of Toronto's biggest entertainment weekly magazine. Her production team, Black Corners, had secured her a record deal through their newly minted imprint with Sony Music, but her deal fell apart when the label closed their Canadian branch. Back at square one, Nobel switched musical gears and wrote music in the vein of the Bad Brains, Blondie, and Prince. She resigned herself to slogging it out by carving out a niche in Canada's music industry.

At the same time, Fefe Dobson, a young biracial singer, blew up the charts with her pop-friendly punk hit "Bye Bye Boyfriend." She hooked up with Chris Smith, Nelly Furtado's manager, and was soon positioned as "the urban Avril Lavigne." She was something unique and different—black but not too black—and her career skyrocketed.

Many music industry insiders I spoke to who were perplexed by the fates of the pair. To many of us it seemed that Fefe Dobson's rock-princess shtick had been manufactured in the studio. In comparison to Nobel's unique blend of alternative rock, punk, and soul, Dobson's radio music seemed completely disposable. Yet she was the black woman playing pop punk who succeeded in breaking the Canadian and, later, the American music markets.

In a 2004 interview with *Observer Music Monthly*, Dobson said that despite her love of rock and punk music, she had great difficulty in getting record labels to see her as anything other than an R&B songstress. "I lived with my [white] mom, a single parent, and I never got any of my dad's heritage," she explained. "So I never understood reggae, or any of that culture. I listened to rock. When I was thirteen, I was going through a depression, trying to deal with who I was."

Dobson was a chosen one, but her success did not spark a tidal wave of signings of black women in punk bands. "What's unfortunate is that it seems like there can't be more than just one black alternative girl," says former Blaxäm front woman Saidah Baba Talibah. "There are so many artists out there that have something burning in them, and that's their music and that's their truth. And then are artists that are manufactured, trying to get somewhere to make that hit and do something trendy. I don't know the ins and outs of what happened with Graph, but there are a whole lot of white indie rock bands that sound the same and they all on the top of the charts."

Dobson's day in the sun appeared to be short-lived, as her 2006 album *Sunday Love* was shelved by her record company days before it was slated for release. She kept busy writing songs for other young female pop artists, and her third album, the mainstream sounding *Joy*, was released in November 2010. Meanwhile, Graph Nobel eschewed the charts altogether and delved deeper into alternative music, working with black alternative rock singer Res and ex–Black Star member Talib Kweli in Idle Warship. For Res's part, her blend of soulful rock never fit into the formats of either rock radio or urban radio. Like Nobel and Dobson after her hit, she struggled to get promotion from her label and got little to no radio airplay.

And that's just the would-be punk stars. Female black guitarists have life even harder. The image of a black male guitarist like Jimi Hendrix or Slash from Guns N' Roses is not as foreign as the image of black female guitarists, such as Toshi Reagon and Tracy Chapman; bluesy hard rock guitarist Suzanne Thomas from Crank and Suzanne & the Blues Church; bassist Meshell Ndegeocello; and Bibi McGill, former guitarist for pop singer Pink and current bandleader for R&B singer Beyoncé. "Women just aren't supposed to have guitars," says Mahon. "There are these rare examples such as Memphis Minnie or Big Mama Thornton who played guitar well and sang, as opposed to the ones who use it as a decoration. But there is no line showing this genealogy between these women who emerged in the 1930s, 1940s, and 1950s and the younger women, like Toshi Reagon or Tracy Chapman or even Tamar-kali. Instead they are seen as an anomaly."

The legendary producer Steve Albini of Nirvana, Neurosis, the Pixies, and Jesus Lizard fame helped Ashley Greenwood and her band Rise from Ashes engineer some demo tracks. "There were a number of male musicians that I know who were very jealous, like: 'How did you get that?' What do you mean, how did I get that? That's why I have to practice longer than the other guitarists, and write more than other guitarists, because I always have to prove myself. That's why I lose my mind when I get onstage. If I don't, they're going to say, 'She sucks,' or suggest I do acoustic or get a fourth guitar to fill in. That's not what I want. I can rock out just as hard as hard as any other guy in a band, but it always seems that at every show I have to prove that I can rock, that I am rock, that this isn't R&B or soul."

Many white women have delivered the goods and made aggressive music, like blues singer Janis Joplin, ex-Runaways shredder Lita Ford, punk singer Wendy O. Williams, German metal icon Doro Pesch, riot grrrl rockers Kat Bjelland and Kathleen Hanna, demon-voiced Arch Enemy singer Angela Gossow, contemporary figures such as Julie Christmas and Courtney Love, and Kylesa guitarist/vocalist Laura Pleasants. Veteran rock journalist Cynthia Dagnal-Myron believes that it would take just one black woman to serve as a pioneer and create a legitimate image for others to follow. "To break through racial and sexual stereotypes," she says, "all you have to do is twist them around and throw them in the face of the audience. There is a tradition of that. Think of the blues women who were not attractive at all, but they sang as hard as men and drank as hard as the men. But you may still be perceived as a novelty."

The BRC's Davis wants to see black audiences come around to embracing metal and punk. "The hurdle that people want to focus on is the black audience not supporting black rock artists," she says. "You see it at the Afro-Punk festivals and tours. People aren't really there for the music as much as they're there for the scene and the cool factor. We just need to get people back into supporting music and musicians, supporting art instead of just supporting the scene."

Mahon suggests that black rock musicians convey the important relationship between harder music and tough, socially relevant messages. Both make people pay attention. "During the disco era," she says, "the music really shifted in terms of promoting more of a lighthearted approach and I think that part of that is how radio stations were selling themselves to advertisers—the lowest common denominator and all of that kind of thing. So rock becomes an important tool as it becomes an important outlet, not just because of the sound and the visual images that people can present but also the lyrical content. There is all this freedom, and an expectation that you can talk about anything, not just girls and cars."

One of the main positives for black women musicians is that by building an online presence and garnering popularity because of your music, there is less emphasis on trying to fit into marketing demographics. Musicians today can simply bypass the labels and market their own music via Twitter, Facebook, and Tumblr. Sites like Bandcamp permit purchase of digital downloads, physical CDs, and new vinyl pressings directly from the artists. SoundCloud and Spotify also allow musicians to post tracks online for streaming to the devices of listeners. Some musicians are creating their own Vimeo or YouTube channels to distribute music videos instead of relying on the major video television stations. Metal and punk fans spend hours online daily, and bands can quickly meet audiences there as large as they could at a big show.

Guitarist Dallas Coyle believes new artists should take online interaction deeper and create and maintain a blog, focusing more on personal experiences and personality. "You start a blog about music and being a musician and you keep that blog going for a year," he says, "and when your music is good enough and you have enough people visiting your blog, then you put the music out there. Focus on yourself first."

Vocalist Talibah made marketing her music online work. Her 2009 release, *The Phone Demos* EP, was, as the name indicates, a demo recording that she released and practically gave away. "It's like something for people to take home and get to know the raw beginnings of the songs," she explains. "Its important to me that listeners are privy to that journey." She also created a loyalty program where people who donate money to help her pay for her studio time would receive a number of personal gifts and services from her.

To build the anticipation for her 2010 album, *Black Bottom*, Tamarkali utilized iTunes and CD Baby to release teaser singles in advance of the album. She offered a number of different versions—album versions, radio edits, remixes—that highlighted her work with artists from other musical genres, such as MC Jean Grae and her all-female string ensemble, the Psychochamber Ensemble. The online marketing of the documentary *Afro-Punk: The Rock 'n' Roll Nigger Experience* succeeded because people who had not yet seen it were able to access information online. Furthermore, the message board gave people a chance to meet other black alternative music fans, who often could not find a group of like-minded friends in their real lives. The early incarnation of the website promoted a DIY perspective—while bands might never make a million bucks, the site convinced many that it was within reach to carve out a niche in the underground scene. The Afro-Punk entity has migrated from its original philosophy of being an online escape for social misfits and has now turned into a marketing brand with its annual festival in Brooklyn, catering to kids of color who are even casual fans of punk and hard rock music and fashion. The *New York Times* wrote an article about such "blipsters," young black hipsters who preferred skating gear and alternative music to baggy pants and hip hop.

Ironically, despite the great opportunity to promote black punk bands, many bands now flying the Afro-punk banner are not that great. In their fervor to promote blacks in punk, the festival promoters supported bands that have not yet put together a coherent musical style and can barely play their instruments. To me, it seems that people who had fantasized about being in a band but were not talented had capitalized on the Afro-punk scene, knowing that if they could quickly put something together, they would be able to get promotion. In short, they would never have cut it in the more demanding metal scene—but realistically, when was the last time having black kids in rock bands was trendy?

"One of the criticisms of the 2008 Afro-Punk Festival was that on one of the days all of the bands had a black singer but all of the rest of the musicians were white," says Davis. "That says to me that we need to get more black folks playing guitars and we need to get more black folks behind drum kits and bass kits playing rock 'n' roll. Not just saying that you like it and support it but actually play it. You just can't go through the motions, like play neo-soul and put the guitar on 2 and try and play a little wah-wah, but you know, actually creating the rock. White kids are still shredding in their bedrooms and black kids aren't necessarily shredding and aren't playing at the level that they should be to be successful."

Though I urge black women to play heavy metal, I understand that this is a terrible time to be encouraging people to try to make a career out of playing in any kind of band. "I think young people want to know what style of music they will need to do to make a living," says Berklee professor Kudisan Kai. "At Berklee, rock seems to be one of the last genres on the curriculum to be considered, and it seems virtually impossible to find female rock musicians on the Berklee campus."

Back to the black press. Black-centric print and online magazines are integral in exposing black artists when well-known, widely distributed publications will not. If radio stations have a hard time placing unique musicians into their formats, at least magazines should cover a better range of musical genres. Urban magazines aren't just about what is going on in the music scene; there is an emotional connection to the publications. Readers treat the primarily black and Latino artists like we personally know them, since, as minorities ourselves, we feel more of a kinship with them, especially those who grew up in the same neighborhoods as we did.

However, I don't expect magazines like *The Source, XXL,* or *Rap Up* to cover rock artists, as their focus is primarily hip hop. "They have no interest in black rock and, honestly, they have that right," says Chaney. "There is nothing to be done about it. It's just unfortunate."

At least *Vibe* has previously covered alternative acts and even black rock musicians and bands such as Fishbone, Res, Kina, and Lenny Kravitz. Also, these musicians incorporated black-centric music—soul, ska, reggae, R&B, and blues—that is more recognized by black listeners than metal, hardcore, or punk. The best writing is emerging online, however, from independent sources. Journalist Blue writes about her personal experiences in the metal scene, on Ectomag.com. Filmmaker Sheila Hardy—Kai's sister—has launched the documentary *Nice and Rough: Black Women in Rock*, and in 2012 launched an accompanying website to promote black women rock and metal artists around the world.

Black extreme music musicians who are influenced by artists like Iron Maiden, Metallica, or Guns N' Roses are rarely even considered "black rock," foremost because their music rarely acknowledges any black musical genres. "It goes back to people being uncomfortable with people trying to merge two musical ideals coming from two races, which is very unfortunate," says Karma Elise, who runs FourteenG.net with Erika Kristen. "Metal is primal and touches that part of your soul that is a little wild and believes in anarchy and all these ideals that have nothing to do with control. It's kind of a thing that you could vicariously live through the music or the lyrics. But if the music goes a little too far, then there is no black identity. So you have the other set of people who come in and say, 'Oh, we need to pull this back. You need to have yours, we need to have our own.'"

Professor and rock journalist Devon Powers also feels that editors of black magazines are also motivated by a survival instinct to control how readers view certain genres of music. "You could say that it's a pure calculation, that because of the information they have from their readers they don't think that their readers are going to be interested in this. These are the kinds of decisions that editors make all the time. But I think that you can also see that those magazines have a very strong interest in a very fragile, but very important, idea of what blackness is. They have a strong interest in it because their very existence depends on it because of separatism."

Black female extreme metal journalists have the power to introduce their readers to new artists, but the artists have to be credible and talented enough to make the cut. Dagnal-Myron admits that being a beautiful young black woman in the late '60s and '70s worked to her advantage, but she was all business. Her mentor, famed writer Lester Bangs, actually warned her to keep her interactions professional, so that musicians would know she was the real deal and not simply there as a groupie.

As a black female journalist covering metal myself, sometimes it seems like there are more haters than supporters. "Just like with most women musicians and fans in metal, you would have to work twice as hard as a guy, that just goes without saying," says Blue. "Even if you take color out of the equation, women in metal have to work harder. And if a white woman has to work twice as hard, a black woman is going to have to work four times as hard. You will ultimately get the same acceptance, but you have to work for it."

Despite having her photos published in print magazines, Kristen still has a hard time getting support from her family and friends. "It wasn't until I would get a photo in a magazine or when my photos were in museums that I would get some sort of nod or some thumbs-up to what I do," she says. "I can sit here and watch Music Choice and see some of my pictures flash across the screen, but to them, it just doesn't mean anything. These people then wonder why I can be distant, and I say, 'This is a part of me, so you are either going to get me or you don't.'"

People around us also don't get how cool the metal experience can be. I took photos in the press pit at a Metallica show, and I was shocked that James Hetfield, Rob Trujillo, and Kirk Hammett stopped and posed for my camera to graciously make sure I got great shots. "It was because you're black, girl!" Kristen laughed. "They know how difficult it is when you have those other photographers out there who are hoping to get that money shot. And you have to speak up and actually articulate how much that meant. As much as you encourage them, they will in turn do that for the next person. You may never cross paths again with these people, but you can thank them and encourage them to make it better for that next person."

Geography can also play a part. Resistance to black women in the metal, hardcore, and punk scenes seems to be prevalent more within North American shores. After all, black artists from jazz musician Nina Simone to esteemed writer James Baldwin found more appreciative audiences overseas. "Europe just does not have the same history of the black struggle as America," says Jingo de Lunch's Yvonne Ducksworth, who lives in Berlin. "Josephine Baker and Eartha Kitt were outspoken black women who were finally treated as the incredible humans they were once they got to Europe."

Even today, singer Tamar-kali says that if she wants to get a decent paid gig, she has to venture out of her Brooklyn digs and head to Europe. "I've had more opportunities there than I have here. I've played Spain, Amsterdam, and France. The thing about it is that most of these shows are just because they said, 'This artist is great. Let's have her.' It's so not what I am used to here. 'Send in this, send in that, try to apply for this and that' versus 'I'm going to pay you and fly you over and give you accommodations.'"

"Tamar is correct," says Sandra St. Victor. The Family Stand singer left New York City for Europe a decade ago. "There are more festivals and venues here with budgets and open audiences. In the U.S., you've got the *Essence* Festival and then there's everything else. Here, there are a plethora of festivals with a varied audience and all kinds of artists. That's one reason Josephine Baker came here back in the day. We've got plenty of cool scenes in the U.S., in New York City, the Bay Area, and in Atlanta. But without budgets, we've got many scenes, but no script! I do believe we're coming into a place where that's changing. I do believe that more people are tired of being part of the herd. The black sheep will take over the field soon enough."

"In the States you are in the position of the beggar. You have to beg for everything. Abroad, people want you," says Tamar-kali. "Straight up. They want what you're bringing; they want to feel the flavor. Part of that is because nobody likes their own news; they always like the 'other.' There are Algerian brothers and sisters and Senegalese people who are catching hell in France, but they love African-Americans. But in general it's a different aesthetic in terms of when people hear something; they don't really have an expectation of what the singer should look like."

Though the numbers are very few, a handful of black females in the music industry are silently showing that the metal, hardcore, and punk scenes are not only exclusively populated and run by young white men. Women like Lunden De'Leon have made seamless transitions into the metal scene. She founded the metal, punk, hardcore, and reggae record label Dirrty Records in Los Angeles in 2003. A model and actress who loved the Dead Kennedys and the Sex Pistols growing up, she was also a metal fan, and saw a dearth of punk and metal labels on the West Coast. Initially, she faced resistance to her focus on those genres. "There were people in my circle who thought that, being a black woman, I should focus on R&B and release sad love songs," she says. "But that wasn't me. I had to be true to myself and do it my way.

"The metal bands in Los Angeles are great," she adds. "At shows in L.A., it's all about the music and not the color of my skin. But down in the Deep South, those rednecks are crazy. I went to a show in South Carolina and I did not feel welcome. The artist who invited me to see them play had no idea I was black. He and the rest of his band acted as if they wanted to see some ID to make sure that I was the owner of Dirrty Records. The South still has a long ways to go."

"There is a certain stigma in American culture about black men and women," says Coyle. "I think that can work against a female black musician, but we are really not going to find out until we find that black female musician [who] can sell that record. I think that the time is not that far off—sometimes you don't know what band it's going to be."

"Women buy music," he adds. "Fourteen-year-old girls are the main record-buying demographic. And because records aren't selling as much, that also begs the question—how is music going to be sold in the future? I think that, regardless of what you look like, there are people who respond to messages more than anything else. What you put on top of that message is what exploits the message or what gets the message to hit home."

The most important advice is to focus on your passion, be realistic about the environment, but never let issues sway you from your dreams. Alexis Brown from Tennessee band Straight Line Stitch is the most visible black female musician in the North American extreme metal scene. "No matter how scared I was I went for it," she says, "I went and I did it. You find ways to do it. I came from humble beginnings, but I put an ad in the paper at this rinky-dink record store: 'singer, looking for a band.' You do that when you have passion, when you really want something. You will find ways to get it. I would say, never stop believing in yourself and never let yourself get in the way. Self-doubt will destroy everything. It's easy to be flipped over when you first get in the game and get your head turned around. Stand firm on who you are and what your ideals are. People naturally want to try to tweak who you are, and that's fine, but when they try to put the pillowcase over your head, that's when you have a problem. Definitely stand firm, be true, and know who you are as a unit."

Erika Kristen adds: "Like with most metal people, I have been some sort of loner. I have never had, at any time of my life, a large number of friends. I've had maybe one or two close friends here and there, but I don't want to subject myself to people who don't get me. I live, drink, eat sleep music. It would be different if I was harming others with it, but I am not. I don't impose my views on other people, I might be a great propagandist, but I just don't. It's just not worth my time. You shouldn't have to stifle any part of yourself to people who claim to like or love you."

Says Tamar-kali: "The only advice I could give is, whatever you do, don't dumb yourself down. Don't be afraid to have eclectic tastes; don't be afraid to have talent. You don't have to oppress other people because you might be more talented or whatever, because the scene sometimes is all about energy and spirit. At the same time, don't be ashamed if you happen to be a really great singer or a really great player. You can still walk humble and have a special gift out of just wanting to be able to contribute; I needed to figure that out at one point.

"Be aware of that slave mentality that comes with a lot of subcultures. This relates to dumbing yourself down, because there are people who are like, 'Only the underground stuff is the best stuff,' and just because someone has the ear of a lot of people doesn't mean that they are crap. It just means that a lot of crap happens to have the ear of a lot of people. I'm a believer that if you have something really special, why shouldn't the world know about it and why shouldn't you get exposure and access to a larger audience? I think that elitism of oppression, where we are trying to have a contest [regarding] who is the most oppressed, who is the most hardcore, the most unpalatable, is silly. There are certain things you shouldn't be against letting yourself express to completion. I love to move, I love to dance: That is just who I am, but it's taken me a long time to just let go and be free."

"An artist really does have to find herself and stick to that," adds St. Victor. "There are no formulas for success, only paths that work for each individual. What works for one probably won't work for another. That's why you've just got to be yourself—everybody else is already taken, anyway!"

Epilogue

WHEN I BEGAN WRITING THIS BOOK, I didn't know any other black women who were metal fans. I made a mental list of the issues I had experienced and wanted to explore. Back then my main concern was whether there were enough black women in the scene to justify putting a book together. I wanted to reassure myself that I wasn't losing my mind! Sure, I was initially drawn to metal simply because it was loud, fast, and exciting. As the years went on, I realized that listening to metal let me temporarily escape reality, and gave me a way to exhale the pent-up anger that had been emotionally crippling me. I wanted to know—do other black women out there react to metal in the same way?

As in mentioned in my introduction, when I told people what I was planning, I received lots of support, but also a lot of smirks and even laughter, accompanied by "You're doing what?" I realized that I'd better dig deep into the subject and cover all the concerns of other black women metal fans in the world, not just my own. Not everyone felt comfortable talking about their lives, anonymously or not. At one point, I was chasing black girls in the subway or on the street if they looked like they dressed the part—had Mohawks, tattoos, and body piercing, or were wearing some punked-out getup or a metal T-shirt. I took down names and e-mail addresses, and sometimes when I made contact, I would be told that they didn't want their name out there as they were unsure of how their friends and family would respond. Some women didn't want to label themselves by the music they were into, or flat-out just did not want to talk about race. I also ran across what I guess I would call posers: women who thought it was cool to dress edgy, but didn't want to look beyond the fashion trend and absorb the philosophies of being a punk or a metalhead.

The replies I got from other black women I encountered and questioned were incredibly similar to my own observations and experiences. Some didn't report any negativity regarding their presence in the scene. Most responses to questions about how people reacted to their presence in the local metal or punk scenes were nuanced with highlights and tense moments, experiences that mirrored my own. Women replied to me via handwritten letters and e-mails, some with wonderful fully fleshed-out responses to my persistent questions. Over the years and even during the editing and revising stages of this book, I have only come up with more and more questions.

In general, the younger generations were drawn to the more popular, current bands like Bullet for my Valentine, Trivium, Opeth, Machine Head, and Suicide Silence, which they found out about from MySpace, Facebook, or other online sites. Women in their thirties and forties were more into classic or extreme metal, ranging from standard fare such as Black Sabbath, Iron Maiden, and Judas Priest, to Napalm Death, Mastodon, Gojira, Rwake, Corrosion of Conformity, Immortal, and Cradle of Filth.

I didn't even know about any black women rock musicians until I was in my late teens. These performers meant a lot to me, as a black girl, in that they acknowledged their sexuality as women in alternative and hard rock, but exhibited control over their bodies in a predominantly white male environment. Instead of being fearful and demure, they were powerful and aggressive. To me, hard rock, metal, and punk music seemed like the perfect soundtrack to letting go and letting the inhibitions that had stifled black women from expressing themselves as sexual, beautiful, and, more importantly, normal women, free.

In Toronto these days, I'm not seeing an increase of black folks at the extreme metal shows, but I do see more black at the large concerts for more established bands like Mastodon and Alice in Chains. At metal festivals like Maryland Deathfest, many people of color come out, perhaps because Baltimore not only has a thriving metal scene, but also because it has a large African-American population. At the South by Southwest music festival in Austin, I've noticed an increase in Latino teenagers at the metal showcases, but not so many black fans.

Regardless of whether black women are actively finding online resources to communicate with each other, there are a few blogs that have started in the past few years, like Black Girl into Heavy Metal (theblackgirlintoheavymetal.blogspot.com) that delves not only into the writer's experience within the metal scene, but features new bands and discusses metal music as a whole. Interviewee Erin Jackson's site, I Hope You Can Handle It (rocknrollsista-thetruth.blogspot.com), discusses her experiences, but also politics and current events. While neither blog is solely focused on metal, they do serve as a window into what is happening among young women who are developing musical and social preferences not based on ethnicity, but reflecting an environment where they have access to a myriad of different cultures, musical styles and experiences.

When you stop and think about it, that doesn't sound so strange—does it?

Appendix:

"What Are You Doing Here?": The Survey

As quoted frequently in the main text of this book, I gleaned a great deal of wide-ranging insight with the help of a questionnaire I circulated surveying habits and attitudes towards music. Many of the responses were very interesting beyond the confines of my narrative, so I've included them here in raw, unmixed form for further understanding.

Do you identify as one or more of the following: female, person of color, or person with a disability?
Yes—85.0%

What is your age?
18-to-25—56.1%
26-to-34—14.6%
35-to-40—22.0%
41-to-50—7.3%

Do you go see bands perform music from your favorite musical genre? If yes, how often? Do you go with a friend?
Yes, I attend about 1 to 10 concerts a year with friends—59.5%
Yes, I attend about 1 to 10 concerts a year by myself—13.5%
Yes, I attend about 11 to 20 concerts a year with friends—8.1%
Yes, I attend about 11 to 20 concerts a year by myself—8.1%
No, I do not attend concerts—18.9%

Where do you meet people that share your music tastes?
Internet/social networking sites (Myspace, Facebook, etc)—65.0%
School—27.5%
Workplace—12.5%
Nightclubs—20%
Music concerts—30%
Through friends and family members—40%

How do you discover new musical artists in your favorite genre?
TV music video channels—23.7%
Music and pop culture magazines—26.3%
Internet message boards—50%
Internet social networks—50%
Word of mouth—50%
Radio—28.9%
Other responses included: iTunes, alternative newspapers, hearing songs at live shows, reading blogs, and satellite radio.

Do people criticize or judge you on your musical preference? If so, please give an example of a specific incident:
—"Some wigger Juggalo said I wasn't a real black person. I hit him in the mouth, then he ran. But other than that it's all good."
—"Yes. I've been told once that I should stop listening to 'funeral music.'"
—"Used to, but now I'm sought after for production work even with hip hop artists. And despite leaning to the electronic side, I have guitar chops. So, I feel like my tastes are respected because of ability."
—"Yes, my students."
—"Yes. Like chavs [UK hooligans]."
—"Yeah. They say it's not modern enough."
—"Yes. Many people say the style of music I like isn't really music, it's

just loud noise. Or that I'm not black because I like rock or punk music."

—"Yeah, especially when I say I like rock. They think it's like devil music, or white music. I find it hilarious. I revel in my musical tastes and find joy wherever I can."

—"Yes. I have friends outside my race that expect me to listen to rap, and they act different towards me because I'm not being what they expect. My family also doesn't understand what's wrong with me. I have two cousins who are half-white, but identify more with being black. I believe it's because of me introducing different music they they also enjoy it."

—"Hell yeah!"

—"People are surprised more than anything else."

—"Not so much now, but when I was growing up, other black kids asked me why I like 'white people's music'."

—"When I was a child, I was teased about being an Oreo [white on the inside and black on the outside]. Now that I'm an adult, and blipsters and nerd hop have hit the mainstream, it kind of removes that."

—"Yes, when I was in high school. It's hard to know looking back if other kids were criticizing me or just in shock."

—"When I was younger, I was criticized for listening to 'white' music and told I was weird; even to the point that people said something was wrong with me for being a black girl listening to rock 'n' roll. Then I learned that black folks actually *created* it. Yeah yeah!"

—"I get teased for my enjoyment of particular American folk artists by my family frequently, but more because my love of them is so strong than because they disapprove of what I listen to."

—"Yes. Many kids from my ethnic background only listened to rap, hip hop, or R&B. There seem to be only small pockets of true musical history knowledge among the youth of all demographics."

—"No, but I think that's because people already expect me to zig where others zag."

—"Nope. They know not to."

Do you have friends from your cultural background that share your musical preferences? If not, why do you think not?

—"No. There is a clique mentality attached to this music, especially where I am from, Nairobi, Kenya. I think it is more geared towards the rich in society and more toward whites. In order to be exposed to this music you must first of all have gone to a school that had kids who listened to it, or you must live in a major city where a few radio and TV stations dedicate a couple of hours per week to some of this music. And still it is very rare to hear metal, industrial, and the like."

—"It wasn't until the song 'Party Like a Rockstar' by the Shop Boyz came out that my friends took an interest in the music I listen to. When rock music became a fashion trend in black America, they started to listen."

—"No. Because I have no friends, and I'm living behind the times."

—"My sister. Other black women I know seem to feel they cannot relate to that kind of music."

—"I don't have many friends from my cultural background that share my taste in music; if they do it's only because of me, and then only one or two songs. I'm not sure why that is, but it could be because I went to an art high school. Everyone there was mixed race, or predominantly white."

—"No, I don't. I grew up in the South and it was very unpopular among black folks to dig hard rock, heavy metal, and punk. For some reason, people aligned 'white music' with skinheads, the Klan, and neo-Nazis. It was misaligned ideology."

—"For a long time, I was the only one. When I moved to New York, I finally met a small group of others who were also black or biracial and dug hard rock and metal. They inspired me to put together 'Anarchists of Color,' a collective of black singers and musicians playing the music that we identified with: Bad Brains, Prince, Rage Against the Machine, Skunk Anansie, etc. Essentially, it was black rockers doing a tribute to black rock."

—"Yes. It is much easier as an adult to meet other black folks who like all types of music."

At what age did you first discover these genres of music?

—"Probably around ten years old."

—"Ten or maybe eleven."

—"My middle to late twenties."

—"Since I was a child, my mother always listened to Tracy Chapman and Sarah McLachlan. As I grew up, I found other genres."

—"I'm pretty sure I gestated to Hendrix and Janis. But I starting singing at age four."

—"I was around 17."

—"My father is an avid record collector. He raised me on rock, and he even introduced me to Living Colour!"

—"When I was seven, I went to see Kiss with my father."

Respondents were asked to name the artists that were integral to sparking their interest in music, and the results really run the gamut from roots rock to classic heavy metal to current-day metal bands:

—Rammstein, Green Day, AC/DC, Offspring, Guns N' Roses, Supertramp, Thelonious Monk, Tribal Tech, Ian Thomas, Led Zeppelin, Metallica, Lorena McKennitt, Cradle of Filth, Nightwish, Queen, Big Brother and the Holding Company, Kozmic Blues Band, Jefferson Airplane, the Doors, the Beatles, Plastic Ono Band, the Rolling Stones, Louis Armstrong, Tina Turner, Thursday, Pantera, Mars Volta, Between the Buried and Me, Black Sabbath, Jimi Hendrix, Pink Floyd, Genesis, Tears for Fears, Duran Duran, Skid Row, Twisted Sister, Whitesnake, Depeche Mode, the Cure, the Smiths, Morrissey, Soundgarden, Nirvana, the riot grrrl movement, Miriam Makeba, Ella Fitzgerald, Mary Lou Williams, the Specials, the English Beat, the Sugar Hill Gang, Whodini, Grandmaster Flash and the Furious Five, Madness, the Clash, Social Distortion, Consolidated, the Pretenders, James Brown, Count Basie, Duke Ellington, the Go-Go's, Echo and the Bunnymen, Gil Scott-Heron, Mahalia Jackson, the Skatalites, B.B. King, and Kiss.

What was it about these bands that initially attracted you? Was it the music? Imagery or artwork? The physical attributes of the musicians?

—"I loved the bass, and how the instruments blended together. It was like walking through a deserted factory filled with rusty machines, and then at the blink of an eye life gets into them and they start working. I had never felt such impact from a song before. The video wasn't bad either."

—"They were actually singing about something other than money, cars, and women, which was new to me since I was raised on hip hop. It was refreshing to find that there are actual musicians that actually have things to say."

—"I liked the passion, the loudness, the lyrics, and the musicianship."

—"For me it was more the sound, and I guess the lyrics. I always knew the lyrics to almost every song. The general feel of the song also."

—"I was attracted by the sounds, the piercing wail of Robert Plant hovering over Bonham's thundering kick. Mick Jagger's peacock strut and his funky delivery made me want to kick some butt. The countless hours spent singing along with Janis Joplin taught me everything a woman needed to know about the journey of the heart. The imagery of the music colored many sad hours of my often dark childhood."

—"It's loud, fast, and ridiculous."

—"I just loved the power of it. The first rock song that got to me was 'Black Dog' by Zeppelin. I was immediately hooked."

—"I have always been attracted to bands with strong frontpersons; big voices, great stage presence, and a very individual look specific to them, a trademark. Freddie Mercury sings into a mic with half the stand attached so it looks like a staff, and he whips out that royal robe. In the Cure, Robert Smith has his fucked-up makeup and hair, and such a melancholy voice that makes me tremble. Metallica's James Hetfield looks like a fucking lumberjack or truck driver or some crap. He has so much bite and power to his words, it's just brutal. All in all, it's the whole package. If it's not there, I get bored with it. Onstage, I like my rock stars to be superheroes."

—"I was interested in new sounds and other cultures. I was also raised in a political household and took life rather seriously. I enjoyed the music, and any imagery that was different—punk, new wave, or traditional dress from other countries. I also secretly had crushes on some of the cute white guys in ska and punk bands, probably because I didn't know any politically minded guys at all when I was younger. Although I was underage, I wanted to do Terry Hall, Mick Jones, and Joe Strummer *really* badly. Not that I wasn't attracted to the black musicians out there, but because I was black I understood that it was okay to talk about those crushes and not okay to admit my Clash crushes."

—"The pure energy."

What are the best qualities of the music you like to listen to (or perform)?

—"I want to feel raw emotion. It has to be loud. *Bass*! Without the bass there is no point to the music. I need to feel swept away."

—"The song as a whole. When the bass line is on track with the drums, and the guitar is right there with the voice, that's what makes for a really good song. If you have a really good music track, people tend to be a little more forgiving if the lyrics suck."

—"The song topics are varied and creative, and it's a pleasure to listen to real drummers and guitarists rather than machines!"

—"I think everybody in our band has a high level of technical proficiency. I like the marriage of the keyboard and guitar. We groove very heavily and intensely. We have really strong melody lines and the songs are fabulous! I love putting a black woman's voice out there and singing rock the way rock used to be, when it was Bessie Smith's music. The heroes of my '60s rock infatuation were putting on a vibe they got from African-Americans in the South doing R&B. It makes sense that I dug it; it makes sense that I sing it. What I don't get is why a sista can't get famous doing it? You'd think after Tina Turner there'd be a whole slew of black women in rock, but the '80s kind of pigeonholed us into a 'sound like Whitney or else' situation."

—"Vocal arrangements and varied time signatures. I mostly tend to like the bands that have a fun groove, but are still unique, even if they are very pop, like Coheed and Cambria."

—"I like tightness, groove, and conviction."

—"Intensity, a sense of rebelliousness, drama or theatricality, but *not* obvious gimmicks. Strong melodies, lyrical finesse, and musicianship."

—"Socially conscious artists with musical talent are always interesting to me. It's more than entertainment, and affects my mood and the decisions I make about entertainment. As a graduate student, I have a very tight budget. If I want to go to any kind of live performance, music or otherwise, I have to be selective. The Saturday before last, a friend had an extra ticket to see the Refugee All Stars from Sierra Leone. It was a wonderful, empowering show, both for the audience and the artists, I think."

—"Lyrics are usually my bag, but I'd like to think I'm pretty well-rounded and take in the whole package."

Do you feel that the music you prefer has impacted your self-confidence and your sexuality?

—"I am comfortable with myself. If you look at hip hop nowadays, it is all about creating a black Barbie illusion in little girls's heads. It seems the more hip hop progressed, the more black women lost themselves and the independence they fought so hard for. With metal, I have had the opportunity to come across women who are comfortable in their own skin; there is no such thing as being a freak, just being an individual."

—"Listening to hip hop made me feel like I was supposed to be some kind of sex object for men. (Though I'm not saying just rap glorifies sex.) Knowing that all music doesn't reflect women in that way made me feel better about myself as a person. I didn't want to be treated as such a thing."

—"I certainly feel that listening to alternative and rock music helps me to acknowledge feelings of anger or frustration that I generally do not express. It is an emotional outlet for me."

—"This music has impacted me greatly. As a dancer, I rely on the counts of the music to help me get through a performance. As a model, I again rely on the music to determine what attitude I should exude. I wasn't always a very confident person, but listening to people like Ani DiFranco has greatly changed my outlook on my sexuality, my confidence, and then some."

—"My feminine idols—Robert Plant, Janis, and Freddy Mercury—were pretty butch, so I think that always made me want to be tough in love. But being born a lesbian made me dig chicks. Then again, when I was a teenager into Mötley Crüe I femmed out, so I guess rock music helped me explore gender expression with confidence."

—"It made me stronger personally, because I knew I would catch some flak for it, and I would have to be willing to explain and stand up for myself."

—"Absolutely. I find hard rock and heavy metal to be very empowering. Sexually—no doubt about it, heavy music gets me off—that's why I love it and live it. But the crap side is the stereotype of a female metalhead; that she is, or should be, slutty. Believe me, every scene has its whores. Male and female stereotypes exist for a reason, but it's *not* the bottom line."

—"I love listening to mid-to-late 20th century female R&B blues artists, because of their humor and sexual confidence. I also admire hip hop artists that present themselves as intelligent, powerful women. I'll never forget how excited I was when I first heard Queen Latifah's *All Hail the Queen*. I have some ideological qualms with Missy Elliott; she has had some artists who have made homophobic statements make cameo appearances on her albums, and I disliked an anti-Asian stereotype that appeared on *The Cookbook*. But I really enjoy her humor and belief in her own beauty and right to be different. I admire Tamar-kali for her bravery and persistence as a black woman punk rock artist. I also admire African women artists for their artistry and their obvious self-acceptance. Angelique Kidjo presents herself without hair weaves. Although I am American, I can relate to her better than I can to Beyoncé. When I listen to political music with progressive messages it is a nice reminder that I am not alone in my interests and concerns."

If you found out that an artist or a member of a group you admired had publicly made a racist or sexist comment, would you:

Immediately boycott them, getting rid of their CDs, etc.?—41.7%

Not let it affect your preference for the music?—41.7%

Just ignore the hype, as it is probably just a rumor?—25.0%

Boycott their music and reevaluate your passion for entire genre. Are they all a bunch of closet racists?—0.0%

Comments?

—"It's not about the band for me. Its about the music."

—"I would try to learn more about the incident. If the person does turn out to be racist, I could not enjoy their music any longer and would get rid of it."

—"I would evaluate the overall situation. After finding out Axl Rose dropped an N-bomb in a song, I lost respect for him as a person, but that doesn't change the importance of his music. In hip hop, artists make racist, sexist, homophobic commentary all the time."

—"It's disappointing, but if their music moved you, you have to appreciate that for what it was and move on."

—"I would need more information about it first. Everybody has some sort of prejudices against somebody. I guess it would depend on how strong the statement was."

—"Now this highly depends on context. If someone said something out of malice, then I can't have them in my collection and have a good conscience."

If you are single, how important is it that a potential mate or current partner share your musical tastes?

Important—41.7%

Not very important—16.7%

Comments?

—"It does help if we do have the same taste."

—"Somewhat important. I'd love to date another African-American, but many of them can't stand my music and believe I don't accept my ethnicity or culture because I don't prefer the Top 40 R&B hits."

—"I am not single. My partner and I have the same tastes in music, and she is from a very strict cultural background. Where I grew up listening to what I felt was classier heavy metal and rock, she listened to the gritty kind. I was a classical romantic Goth. She was a crowd-surfing and moshing rock chick."

—"I'm not single and I like a wide variety of music. My wife's taste overlaps my own."

—"I'm a music lover in general. Sometimes learning about other genres is a good thing, but the other person has to be passionate about good music."

—"They have to *get it*. Thankfully my husband likes rock—not always the same bands, but he understands why I like what I do."

—"That's somewhat important, because it's such a big part of me and they are gonna be hearing *a lot* of it!"

—"It's nice, but not essential. It would be nice to enjoy the music together."

How important is the music you perform or listen to in your daily life?
Music keeps me sane; I listen to it all day—83.3%
Music is a hobby; my real life is more important—0.0%
I just listen to music; I don't participate in the culture—0.0%
Not important; I just listen to music because my partner does—16.7%
Comments?
—"Music keeps me sane and influences certain aspects of my life, but it is not like it is a religion for me."

—"I *love* my music. I have very eclectic tastes. I listen to music before I go to sleep, I play it in my car, and I wear earphones at work. My iPod goes to the gym with me, and I have playlists on my web sites. But it's a solitary affair. I won't hang out with young white male hetero rockers!"

—"I have music in the morning to get dressed by; after school and work to wind down; and sometimes as a break during the day!"

—"I do have days where I listen to absolutely nothing. Everyone needs quiet time."

Bibliography

INTRODUCTION

Bangs, Lester. "The White Noise Supremacists," *The Village Voice*, April 30, 1979.

Chaney, Keidra. "Sister Outsider Headbanger," *Bitch Magazine*, 2000.

Tate, Greg. Foreword for *Rip it Up: The Black Experience in Rock n' Roll*. Edited by Kandia Crazy Horse (Palgrave, 2004).

I. CANADIAN STEEL

"Black Punk Time: Blacks in Punk, New Wave, and Hardcore 1976–1983 (Part 1)," *Rocktober* #32, 2002.

Gutmann, Amy. "Responding to Racial Injustice," *Color Conscious: The Political Morality of Race*, (Princeton: Princeton University Press, 1996).

Collins, Patricia Hill. *Black Feminist Thought: Knowledge, Consciousness, and the Politics of Empowerment* (New York: Routledge, 2000).

Who Gets In? (documentary*)*, National Film Board of Canada, 1998.

II. METAL CAN SAVE YOUR LIFE (OR AT LEAST YOUR SANITY)

"Effects of Listening to Heavy Metal Music on College Women: A Pilot Study," College Student Journal, (March 2008).

Walser, Robert. *Running With the Devil: Power, Gender, and Madness in Heavy Metal Music* (Wesleyan, 1993).

III. I'M HERE BECAUSE WE STARTED IT!

Crazy Horse, Kandia. "Interview with Venetta Fields," from *Rip it Up: The Black Experience in Rock n' Roll*. Edited by Kandia Crazy Horse (Palgrave, 2004).

Dawes, Laina. "Everything but the Burden: An Interview with Author and Cultural Theorist Greg Tate," Afropunk.com, September 20, 2005.

DuBois, W.E.B. "Of Our Spiritual Strivings," from *The Souls of Black Folks* (2ed.) (Bartleby, 1999).

Ellis, Trey. "The New Black Aesthetic" from *Callaloo* (journal) No. 38, 1989.

Goldman, Vivien. "Blues for Betty Davis's Smile: The Betty Davis Lacuna," from *Rip it Up: The Black Experience in Rock n' Roll*. Edited by Kandia Crazy Horse (Palgrave, 2004).

McNeill, Darrell M. "Rock, Racism, and Retailing 101: A Blueprint in Cultural Theft," from *Rip it Up: The Black Experience in Rock n' Roll*. Edited by Kandia Crazy Horse (Palgrave, 2004).

Walser, Robert. *Running With the Devil: Power, Gender, and Madness in Heavy Metal Music* (Wesleyan, 1993).

Who Gets in? (documentary), National Film Board of Canada, 1998.

IV. SO YOU THINK YOU'RE WHITE?

Chaney, Keidra. "Sister Outsider Headbanger," *Bitch Magazine*, 2000.

Collins, Patricia Hill. "The Power of Self-Definition," from *Black Feminist Thought: Knowledge, Consciousness and the Politics of Empowerment* (New York: Routledge, 2000).

Davis, Angela Y. *Blues Legacies and Black Feminism* (New York: Vintage Books, 1999).

Gutmann, Amy. "Responding to Racial Injustice," from *Color Conscious: The Political Morality of Race* (Princeton: Princeton University Press, 1996).

V. "The Only One" Syndrome

Afro-Punk: The Rock n' Roll Nigger Experience (documentary). 2003. James Spooner (director).

Dawes, Laina. "Interview with Animals as Leaders' Toshin Abasi," *Exclaim! Canada*, November 21, 2011.

VI. Too Black, Too Metal, and All Woman

Alexander, Elizabeth, *The Venus Hottentot*, University Press of Virginia, Callaloo Poetry Series, 1990. Reissued by Graywolf Press, 2004.

Collins, Patricia Hill. "The Sexual Politics of black Womanhood," from *Black Feminist Thought: Knowledge, Consciousness and the Politics of Empowerment* (New York: Routledge, 2000).

Dawes, Laina. "Psychology Today: 'Black Women Less Attractive than Other Women'...and Plants and Animals, Too," Blogher.com, May 18, 2011.

Heavy Metal Parking Lot (documentary). John Heyn and Jeff Krulik (directors). 1986.

Hunt, Marsha. *Undefeated* (Greystone Books, 2006).

Interview, Skin and Brian Tufano, Thespaceuk.com.

Leseman, Linda. "Dave Mustaine's Advice for Starving Women in Africa: 'Put a Plug in It'," *LA Weekly*. February 23, 2012.

Mahon, Maureen. *Right To Rock: The Black Rock Coalition and the Cultural Politics of Race* (Duke University Press, 2004*).*

Nixon, Chris. "Pinkett Smith gets 'Wicked'," *San Diego Union-Tribune*, February 24, 2006.

Robinson, Knox. "Tamar-kali is Hardcore More Than a Little Bit," *the Fader*, Issue 22, 2003.

Weinstein, Deena. *Heavy Metal: The Music and Its Culture,* Revised Edition (Da Capo Press, 2000).

"Wicked Wisdom Persevering on Ozzfest," *Billboard.com,* July 25, 2005.

VII. The Lingering Stench of Racism in Metal

Davisson, Justin. "Extreme Politics and Extreme Metal: Strange Bedfellows or Fellow Travellers?" Paper presented at Metal Fundamentalisms Conference, November 3-5, 2008, Salzburg, Austria.

Eylon, Lilli. "The Controversy Over Richard Wagner," the Jewish Virtual Library.

Johnson, Jeff. "Don't Blame Hip hop for Society's Sexism," CNN.com, May 7, 2007.

Lee, Cosmo. "Interview: Phil Anselmo."

"Pantera Singer Apologizes for Racial Tirade," *The Montreal Gazette,* March 9, 1995.

"'Vlad the Impaler Was a Genius': The Crazed and Hate-Filled 'Manifesto' of the Mass Murderer," *The Daily Mail* UK, July 25, 2011.

"War in Europe: Part I—Cui Bono?" from Burzum.org.

VIII. Remove the Barricades—and Stagedive!

Bialik, Carl. "Is the Conventional Wisdom Correct In Measuring Hip Hop Audience?," *Wall Street Journal,* May 5, 2005.

Dawes, Laina. "Interview with Graph Nobel," *Numb,* Spring 2006.

"Deejay's Appeal: 'Kill the Whiteness Inside'," *Washington Post,* August 26, 2005.

"Ghetto Fabulous Parties," *XXLMag.com,* January 26, 2007.

Fefe Dobson interview, *Observer Music Monthly,* February 22, 2004.

McNeill, Darrell M. "Rock, Racism and Retailing 101: A Blueprint in Cultural Theft," from *Rip it Up: The Black Experience in Rock n' Roll.* Edited by Kandia

Crazy Horse (Palgrave, 2004).

Pressler, Jessica. "Truly Indie Fans?," *the New York Times*, January 28, 2007.

"U.S. Album Sales Fall 12.8% in 2010, Digital Tracks Eke Out 1% Gain," *Billboard.com*, January 5, 2011.

Weingarten, Christopher R. "The Long Slow Death of Lil Wayne's Rebirth," *Village Voice*, February 2, 2010.

Biographies

SCOTT ALISOGLU is the co-founder of Clawhammer PR, a Topeka-based full service music promotion and media relations company specializing in heavy metal and hard rock. More: www.facebook.com/clawhammerpr

SAMEERAH BLUE is a metal journalist who runs *Ecto Mag*, a metal webzine based in Glendale, CA. More: www.ectomag.com

ALEXIS BROWN is the singer for Knoxville, TN, band Straight Line Stitch. More: www.facebook.com/straightlinestitch

KEIDRA CHANEY is a digital strategy and analytics specialist, a music journalist, a die-hard metalhead, and the bassist and vocalist for Sole Heiress, a two-woman synth/rock band from Chicago. More: keidrachaney.com

MONIQUE CRAFT is a hardcore and metal fan and chef from Newburgh, NY.

DALLAS COYLE is the multi-instrumentalist behind Genetic; the co-founder and former guitarist and vocalist for New Jersey's God Forbid; and the co-founder of Mad Carousel, a production company, art collective, and intellectual property archive. More: madcarousel.com/genetic

LaRonda Davis is the national president for the Black Rock Coalition. More: www.blackrockcoalition.org.

Lunden De'Leon is an actor, producer, and owner and CEO of the punk and metal label Dirrty Records in Los Angeles. She also owns and runs Palmetto Film Studios. More: dirrtyrecords.com

Camille Douglas is a New Orleans-raised singer who currently fronts New York City-based "Rock Roll & Soul" group Empire Beats. More: empirebeatsnyc.com.

Earl Douglas is the executive director of the New York City chapter of the Black Rock Coalition. More: www.blackrockcoalition.org

Yvonne Ducksworth is an original member of Jingo de Lunch. She was previously the vocalist for Manson Youth and Combat Not Conform. Jingo de Lunch's most recent recording is 2010's *Land of the Free-ks*. Raised in Canada, Ducksworth currently resides in Berlin. More: www.jingo-de-lunch.com

Karma Elise is a metal journalist and the co-founder of FourteenG.net, a Chicago-based metal webzine. She currently resides in Göteborg, Sweden. More: www.fourteeng.net

Raymond Gayle is a Houston filmmaker. His first feature-length documentary is *Electric Purgatory: The Fate of the Black Rocker*. More: www.electricpurgatory.com

Ashley Greenwood is the guitarist and vocalist for New Jersey's Rise From Ashes. More: www.myspace.com/risefromashes

ERIN JACKSON is a metal fan and writer who runs the music culture blog I Hope You Can Handle It. More: rocknrollsista-thetruth.blogspot.com

TAMAR-KALI is a guitarist and vocalist from Brooklyn. She is the founder of the Psychochamber Ensemble and the Pseudoacoustic Siren Songs project. She was featured in the 2003 documentary *Afro-Punk,* and her music is featured in the 2011 film, *Pariah.* In 2010 she released her debut full-length, *Black Bottom.* More: www.tamar-kali.com

ERIKA KRISTEN is a photographer, metal journalist, and co-founder of FourteenG.net, a metal webzine. More: www.erikakristen.com

MASHADI MATABANE is not a musician. She is a Ph.D. candidate in American Studies at Emory University in Atlanta. She is also a born-again Southerner and bicultural black woman with a hint of an Afro-indie aesthetic about her. Her dissertation is a cultural history about black women electric guitarists in U.S. popular music. She maintains a blog, Steely Dames, a digital humanities project that provides a growing online archive of black women's use of the electric and acoustic guitars. More: www.steelydames.blogspot.com

MAUREEN MAHON, Ph.D., is an associate professor in the New York University Department of Anthropology. She is the author of *Right To Rock: The Black Rock Coalition and the Cultural Politics of Race* (Duke University Press, 2004). Her current research on the music and legacy of black women in rock examines the intersection of gender, race, sexuality, and music production. More: www.anthropology.as.nyu.edu/object/Maureen_Mahon.html

URITH MYREE is the bassist and backing vocalist for the New York-based all-female hard rock/metal band Dormitory Effect. More: dormitoryeffect.com

CYNTHIA DAGNAL-MYRON is a former reporter for the *Chicago Sun-Times* and the *Arizona Daily Star*. Her reviews and interviews have also appeared in *Rolling Stone*, *Creem* and the English rock magazine *The Word*. She is the author of two books about the music industry. Her next book, *The Keka Collection*, will feature popular posts from her Open Salon blog. She resides in Tucson, AZ.

JASON NETHERTON is the founder, bassist, and vocalist for Baltimore death metal/grindcore band Misery Index. He is currently a Ph.D. candidate at Western University in Ontario. More: www.facebook.com/miseryindex

LAURA NICHOLLS frequented the Toronto punk scene in the 1980s. She went on to obtain her MFA at the American Conservatory Theatre in San Francisco, and is currently an event planner in Toronto.

"PISSO" is a graduate student from Chicago.

DEVON POWERS, Ph.D., is an assistant professor in the Department of Culture and Communication at Drexel University in Philadelphia. She is a former columnist for Popmatters.com. Her book *Sounding Off: The Village Voice and Rock Criticism* is forthcoming in 2013 from the University of Massachusetts Press. More: www.devonpowers.com

DIAMOND ROWE is the lead guitarist for Atlanta-based metal thrashers Tetrarch. More: www.facebook.com/tetrarchga

Deborah Anne Dyer, aka SKIN, is the singer and songwriter for alternative rock/punk/metal band Skunk Anansie. Based in London, in 2009 the band regrouped after a nine-year hiatus. Their studio album *Black Traffic* was released in September 2012. More: www.skunkanansie.net

SANDRA ST. VICTOR is the singer for New York-based rock/soul/funk trio The Family Stand. The band has released six albums. Their latest, *In a Thousand Years*, was released in 2010. St. Victor is also a solo artist, and she currently resides in Amsterdam. More: thefamilystand.bandcamp.com

SAIDAH BABA TALIBAH, a Canadian-born singer, was part of the influential Toronto-based, hard rock/funk group Blaxäm in the mid-'90s. She is now an accomplished solo artist. Her debut album, *(S)Cream*, was released in the fall of 2011. More: www.sbtmusic.com

MILITIA VOX is is a solo artist, as well as the lead singer, songwriter, and matriarch of edgy, original hard rock band Swear on Your Life. She is also known as the frontwoman of New York-based all-girl Judas Priest tribute band Judas Priestess. She has hosted shows and and worked as a VJ for Much Music USA, MTV2, VH1, and "Heavy Metal Makeover" on FUSE TV. More: www.militiaismyname.com

Also Available from Bazillion Points:

METALION: The Slayer Mag Diaries
by Jon "Metalion" Kristiansen
744pp giant hardcover

Best Music Books of 2011, NPR
"744 pages of rabid frankness"—*NY Times*
"Essential reading"—*Vice Literary*

SWEDISH DEATH METAL
by Daniel Ekeroth
448pp softcover

Starred review, *Publishers Weekly*
"Vastly entertaining"—*Time Out*

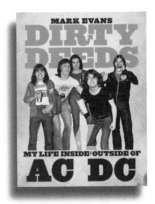

HELLBENT FOR COOKING:
The Heavy Metal Cookbook
by Annick "Morbid Chef" Giroux
224pp deluxe softcover

"Part global cookbook, part underground
metal compendium"—*New York Post*
10 Best Musical Cookbooks, Flavorpill

DIRTY DEEDS:
My Life Inside/Outside of AC/DC
by Mark Evans
288pp softcover

"Rewarding...sincere"—*Library Journal*
"Meaty...plenty of details"—*Gibson.com*
Top 15 of 2011, *Guitar World*

The first and last words in heavy reading.

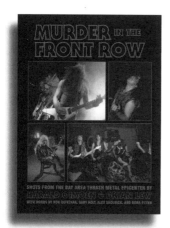

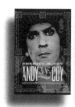